ESTHER'S EDIBLES

RECIPES for COOKING and LIVING

By —
Esther W. Pyle

Esther's Edibles:
Recipes for Cooking and Living

Copyright © 1998 Esther W. Pyle

All Rights Reserved
No part of this book may be reproduced, stored in a retrieval system, or transmitted in any form or by any means—electronic, mechanical, photocopy, recording, or otherwise—without written permission of the publisher, except for brief quotations in printed reviews.

Published by
Emerald House Group, Inc.
1 Chick Springs Road, Suite 206
Greenville, SC 29609 USA

and

Ambassador Productions
16 Hillview Avenue
Belfast, Northern Ireland
BT5 6JH

Dedication

This book is dedicated to the grand ladies who over the past 40 years have entertained my preacher husband and me in their homes. We could never name all of you who have been so kind and thoughtful to us!

We have tasted some of the best food in the land and I am grateful for all I have learned about cooking from the wonderful cooks in our churches.

In the many exciting years as a pastor's wife we had the honor of having many of God's choice preachers and missionaries in our home and at our table. Now travelling for these nearly 10 years on the revival road, the tables have been turned. We are so thankful for all the food and fellowship we have enjoyed through the years.

So, here is a collection of tempting recipes from many places over the United States and two foreign countries. I give credit when I can, but in many cases I failed to jot down the names of the dear ladies who gave them to me. So, if yours is here without your name please forgive me and thank you anyway!

My husband pushed me into this book! I hope you enjoy it.

Esther Pyle
Proverbs 3:5+6

Table of Contents

Beverages:
- Iced Tea — 2
- 7-up punch — 3
- Spiced tea — 4
- Instant spiced tea — 5
- Frozen Banana Punch — 6

Breads:
- Banana Nut Bread — 10
- Hot Corn Bread — 12
- Zucchini-Oatmeal Muffins — 13
- Maple-nut Coffee Twist — 14
- Zucchini Bread — 16
- Pumpkin Bread — 17
- Raisin Bran Muffins — 18
- Cheese Biscuits — 19
- Savory Casserole Bread — 20
- Hush Puppies — 21

Meats:

- Chicken Broccoli Casserole — 24
- Chicken and Yellow Rice — 25
- Chicken Wiggle — 26
- Easy Oven Roast — 28
- Chicken Parmesan — 29
- Crock Pot Steak — 30
- Tasty Salmonettes — 31
- Scalloped Oysters — 32
- Chicken in a stuffing nest — 33
- Impossible Tuna Pie — 34
- Swiss Steak Quickie — 35
- Southern Chicken and Dressing — 36
- "Stuff" — 38
- Chicken Casserole — 39
- Hamburger Stroganoff — 40
- Savory Shrimp — 41
- Porcupine Meat Balls — 42
- Marzetti — 43
- Green Chilies Casserole — 45
- Chicken Corn Soup — 46
- Shake and Bake for Chicken — 47
- Company Chicken — 48

Chicken Every Sunday —————— 49
Green Chili Enchiladas ————— 50
Golden Ham Pie ——————— 52
Southern Fried Chicken ———— 53
Stuffed Camel ——————— 54

Salads:
Carrot and Orange Salad ————— 56
Apricot Jello Salad ————— 57
Strawberry Jello Salad ———— 58
Esther's Potato Salad ————— 60
Shrimp Salad ——————— 65
Lemon Jello Salad ————— 66
Lemon Blueberry Salad ————— 67
Fruit Salad ——————— 68
Tuna Fish Salad ——————— 69
Chicken Salad ——————— 70
Three Bean Salad ————— 71
Make Ahead Vegetable Salad ———— 73
Salad Supreme ——————— 74
Taco Salad ——————— 75
Freezer Coleslaw ————— 76
Conch Salad ——————— 78

Sweet Sour Bean Salad _____ 79
Cranberry Salad _____ 80

Vegetables:
   Turnip Greens _____ 82
   Southern Fried Corn_____ 83
   Sweet Potato Casserole _____ 84
   Green Rice _____ 85
   Company Potatoes _____ 86
   Broccoli Casserole _____ 88
   Fried Okra- _____ 89
   Rice Casserole _____ 90
   Broccoli Casserole _____ 91
   Beets and Pineapple _____ 93
   Eggplant Casserole _____ 94
   Peas and Rice _____ 95
   Macaroni and Cheese _____ 96
   Potato Casserole _____ 97
   Squash Souffle _____ 98
   Rutabagas and Apples _____ 99
   Quick Creamed Spinach ____ 100
   Hash Brown Potato Casserole -- 101
   Asparagus Casserole _____ 103

Shoe Peg Corn Casserole ——————104
Butterbeans, Peas and Okra ——————105

Desserts:
Buttermilk Pie ———————— 108
Downtowner Fudge Pie ——————— 109
Instant Pumpkin Pie ——————— 110
Holiday Fruit Cookies ————— 112
Cheese Ball ———————— 113
Molasses Cookies —————— 114
Fruit Pizza ——————— 115
Apple Slices ———————— 116
Chocolate Peanut Butter Dessert —— 117
Fairy Pie ———————— 118
Blackberry Cobbler ——————— 119
Banana Split Pie ——————— 120
Lemon Cheese Bars ——————— 121
Angel Pie ———————— 122
Orange Delight ——— ————. 123
Rasberry Delight ———————— 124
Cherry Delight ——————— 125
Southern Pecan Pie ———————126
Sisties' Pie ————————127

 Butternut Cake __ _ _ _ _ _. 129
 Pineapple Upside-down Cake _ _ _ 130
 Prune Cake _ _ _ _ _ _ _ 131
 Red Velvet Cake _ _ _ _ _ 132
 Fresh Apple Cake _ _ _ _ _. 133
 Golden Fruit Cake _ _ _ _ _ 135
 Lane Cake _ _ _ _ _ _ _ 136
 Pumpkin Cake Roll _ _ _ _ _ 138
 Sour Cream Cake _ _ _ _ _ 139
 Plum Cake _ _ _ _ _ _ _ 140
 Carrot Cake _ _ _ _ _ _ 141
 Coconut Pound Cake _ _ _. 142
 Lemon Chess Pie _ _ _ _ _ 143
 Chocolate Cake _ _ _ _ _. 144
 Pound Cake _ _ _ _ _ _ 146
 Coconut Cake _ _ _ _ _. 147
 Poor Mans' Cake _ _ _ _ _ 149
 Pea-Pickin' Cake _ _ _ _ _ 150

Pickles and Preserves:
 Bread and Butter Pickles _ _ _ _ . 151
 Pear Relish _ _ _ _ _ _ _ 152

Ode to a Housewife

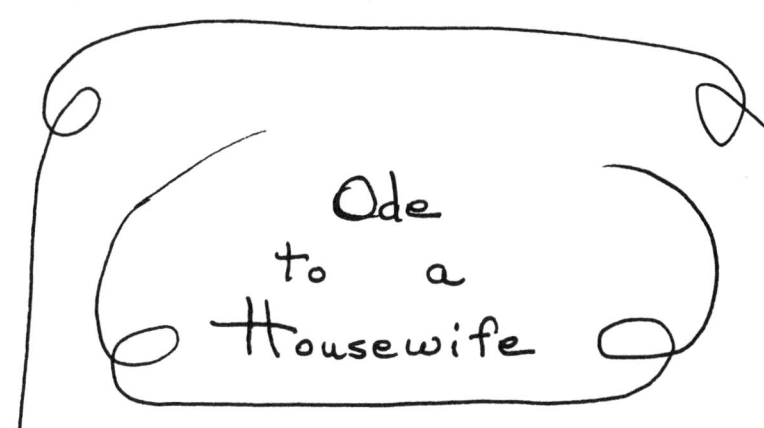

To love and honor are okay,
And one might promise to obey;
But what makes wives turn slowly gray
Is what to cook each blessed day!

Southern Iced Tea

Down south we always have a pitcher of iced tea in the refrigerator! I learned to make <u>real</u> <u>southern</u> iced tea from my dear friend Eva Greenwood in Pensacola, Fla.

In a stainless steel pan bring 1½ to 2 cups of water to a boil. Add 1 family sized tea bag or equivalent loose tea. Turn off the heat and let this steep 15-20 min. Pour tea into a 2 qt. pitcher and add ¾ cup sugar. Add cold water to the tea bag and squeeze out into pitcher. Fill pitcher with cold water. Now you're ready to add ice and enjoy a glass of tea!

7-up Fruit Punch

3 qts. unsweetend pineapple juice
1 6 oz. can lemon juice (diluted)
1 6 oz. can frozen orange juice (diluted)
½ cup sugar
1 pint fresh or frozen strawberries quartered
12 bottles of 7-up

Combine fruit juices, sugar and chill thoroughly.

Just before serving add 7-up and strawberries. Pour over large cake of ice in punch bowl. Float thin slices of lemon or lime.

Serves 65

Spiced Tea

1 tsp. whole cloves
3 sticks cinnamon

Tie spices in a clean cloth – Put in 1 qt. boiling water – boil 5 minutes.

Remove from heat and add 5 tea bags – steep 5 min.

While tea is steeping mix:
1 can orange juice
3 cans water
1 cup sugar

Remove spices and tea bags and add to orange juice mixture and heat.

This is a good hot drink on a cold winter day!

Instant Spiced Tea

C. Neuhardt — Burbank, Ill.

1 cup instant tea
2 cups tang
2 cups sugar
1-2 pkgs. lemonade mix
1 tsp. cinnamon
1 tsp. cloves

Mix these ingredients and put into a jar.

Use 2 tsp. of the mix to 1 cup hot water.

This is nice to have on the shelf for a quick cup of tea.

"Keep thy heart with all diligence; for out of it are the issues of life."
                Proverbs 4:23

Frozen Banana Punch

Zelma Frost, P.C., Fl.

6 bananas (mashed)
6 cups water
4 cups sugar
1 large can pineapple juice
24 oz. frozen orange juice

Boil water and sugar 3 min. Add rest of ingredients and freeze in 3 containers.

Add 1-32 oz. 7-up to each. This makes a slush.

"In my Father's house are many mansions: if it were not so, I would have told you. I go to prepare a place for you."

John 14:2

Jesus

Others

Yourself

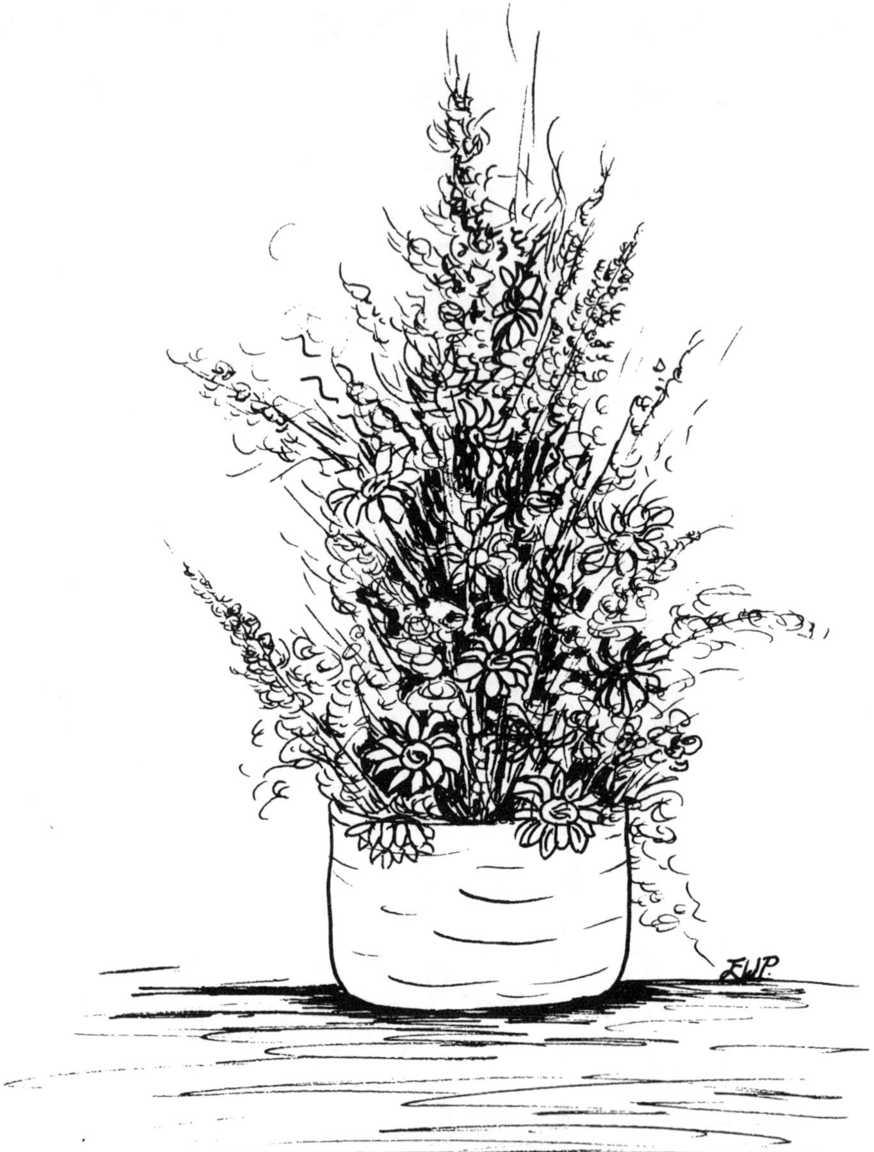
EWP.

BREADS

"Jesus said unto them, I am the bread of life: he that cometh to me shall never hunger, and he that believeth me shall never thirst."

— John 6:35

Banana Nut Bread

2 cups sifted flour
2 tsp. baking powder
1 tsp. salt
½ tsp. soda
1 cup sugar
½ cup butter or margarine
2 eggs
1 cup mashed bananas
1 tsp. lemon juice
1 cup chopped nuts

    Sift together flour, B.P., salt, soda, and sugar. Add shortening, eggs, bananas and lemon juice. Stir to combine ingredients, then beat 2 min. at med. speed on mixer. Stir in ¾ cup nuts.
    Pour into greased loaf pan 5¼ x 9½ inches
Sprinkle rest of nuts on top.
Bake at 350° 1 hour and 15 min.

Ingredients for a Happy Home

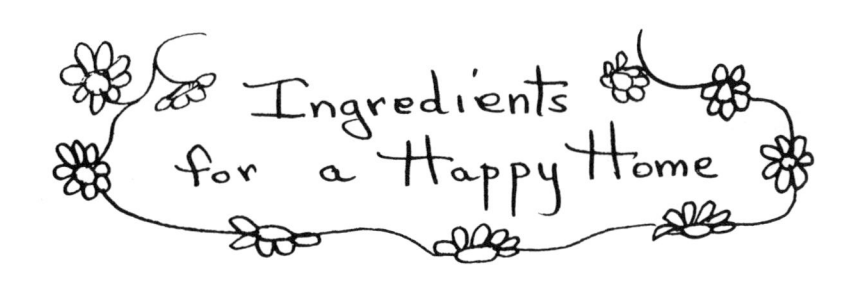

1 — Planning — Proverbs 14:1

2 — Simplicity — Proverbs 15:27

3 — Quietness — Proverbs 17:1
　　　　　　　　Proverbs 21:9

4 — Forgiveness — Proverbs 17:13

5 — Understanding — Proverbs 24:3

6 — Determination — Proverbs 24:27

7 — Godliness — Matt. 7:24, I Cor. 3:11

Hugh F. Pyle

Hot Corn Bread

Edna King P.C., Fl.

1 cup grated cheese
1 small can cream corn
1 cup corn meal
1 tsp. salt
½ tsp. soda
2 eggs
2 finely chopped hot peppers
¾ cup buttermilk
½ cup wesson oil

Mix and bake in 350° oven.

Good with fresh vegetables!

"I have seen servants upon horses, and princes walking as servants upon the earth."
Ecclesiastes 10:7

Zucchini-Oatmeal Muffins

Joan Twedell, Colo.

2½ cups flour
1½ cups sugar
1 cup pecans
½ cup quick oats (uncooked)
1 tsp. B.P.
1 tsp. salt
1 tsp. cinnamon
4 eggs
1 med. zucchini (shredded)
¾ cup salad oil

Preheat oven to 400°.
Into a large bowl measure first 7 ingredients. In medium bowl with fork beat eggs slightly. Stir in oil and zucchini. Stir all at once into flour mixture until moistened.

Spoon into 15-16 muffin tins, greased.

Bake 25 minutes

Maple-nut Coffee Twist

New Jersey — Barbara

A pastors wife gave this to me years ago and it has become a tradition for Christmas morning breakfast when the family gets together.

- 1 Pkg. Pillsbury hot roll mix
- 3/4 cup warm water
- 1 egg
- 3 Tbsp. sugar
- 1 tsp. maple flavoring
- 6 Tbsp. melted butter

Filling

- 1/2 cup sugar
- 1 tsp. cinnamon
- 1 tsp. maple flavoring
- 1/2 cup chopped nuts

} Combine

Glaze

- 1 1/2 cups confectioners sugar
- 1/2 tsp. maple flavoring
- 2 or 3 tsp. milk

Directions:

In a large mixing bowl, dissolve yeast in warm water. Stir in egg, sugar, and maple flavoring. Add the flour mixture; blend well. Knead on a floured surface 2 or 3 minutes until smooth and satiny. Place in a greased bowl. Cover; let rise in a warm place until light and doubled in size. (30-45 minutes.)

Prepare filling ⌒ then —

Divide dough equally into 3 balls. On lightly floured surface roll out one ball of dough to 12 in. circle. Fit onto bottom of 12 inch pizza pan. Brush dough with 2 tbsp. melted butter and sprinkle with about ⅓ cup of the filling. Continue in the same manner, forming 2 more layers and ending with filling. Use a glass to mark a 2 in. circle in center of dough (do not cut through dough). Cut from outside edge just to circle forming 16 pie-shaped wedges. Twist each of the 3 layered wedges 5 times. Let rise in a warm place until light and doubled in size, (30-45 minutes)

Bake at 375° for 20 to 25 minutes until golden brown. Drizzle with glaze while still warm.

Sometimes I make these in 3 layers and cut it up like a coffee cake.

Zucchini Bread

Nancy Sills

3 eggs
2 cups sugar
1 cup vegetable oil
2 cups raw, peeled zucchini

3 tsp. vanilla
3 cups flour
1 tsp. salt
1 tsp. soda

3 tsp. cinnamon
¼ tsp. B.P.
1 cup chopped nuts

Beat eggs until light and foamy, add sugar, oil, grated zucchini, and vanilla.

Mix dry ingredients and add to egg mixture.

Stir until blended, and add nuts.

Bake 1 hour at 350°.
Makes 2 loaves.

Faith makes all things possible,
Hope makes all things bright,
Love makes all things easy.

Pumpkin Bread
Wynell Ropke

3½ cups flour (self-rising)
1 tsp. cin.
1 tsp. nutmeg
3 cups sugar
2 eggs
1 cup cooking oil
⅔ cup water
2 cups pumpkin (1 can)
½ cup pecans

Sift dry ingredients into bowl. Add all remaining ingredients. Mix until smooth. Bake in 3 greased and floured loaf pans for about 45 min. in 350° oven.

The secret of happiness is not to do what you like to do, but to learn to like what you have to do!

Raisin-Bran Muffins

Mrs. Walter Hughes, Canada

1 cup raisin bran } let stand
1 cup milk

Then add:
1 beaten egg
½ cup sugar
⅓ cup oil
1 cup self-rising flour
   (add nuts if desired)

Mix together and bake in muffin tin for 10-15 min. at 400°.

Makes about 15 muffins.

"The blessing of the Lord, it maketh rich, and he addeth no sorrow with it."
            Proverbs 10:22

Cheese Biscuits

Jean Smith — Panama City, Fl.

½ lb. butter
½ lb. cheese

Cream butter, Grate cheese and cream together.

Sift together:
2 cups flour
1 tbsp. sugar
½ tsp. paprika

Sift flour mixture into butter and cheese.

Form small balls and place on ungreased cookie sheet. Press each down with pecan half.

Bake 30 min. in 350° oven until biscuit can be picked up without crumbling.

"A friend loveth at all times."
Proverbs 17:17

Savory Casserole Bread

2/3 cups chopped green onions (or 1/3 cup dried)
2 cups Bisquick mix
1 cup chopped cooked ham or corned beef
2 eggs slightly beaten
2/3 cups milk
1/2 tsp. prepared mustard
1 1/2 cups grated sharp cheddar cheese
2 Tbsp. sesame or dill seed
3 Tbsp. melted butter or margarine

    Saute onions in Tbsp. oil about 2 minutes. Combine Bisquick mix and ham. Mix remaining oil, eggs, milk, mustard, onion and half the cheese. Add to ham mixture; stir well.

    Spread in round greased 10 inch casserole 1 to 1 1/2 inches deep.

    Sprinkle with remaining cheese and seed, then pour butter over top.

    Bake at 375° for 35-40 min.

    Cut in wedges and serve hot.

Hush Puppies

Eula Palmer, P.e., Fl.

1 cup self-rising corn meal
½ cup self-rising flour
1 small onion chopped
1 tsp. soda
1 egg
buttermilk

Mix dry ingredients thoroughly. Add egg and onion. Slowly stir in just enough buttermilk to make a thick batter. Drop by teaspoon in hot fat (about 375°) until they are golden. They will turn themselves over.

Southeners fry hushpuppies along with fish. This was originally done to keep the dogs quiet during a fish fry.

forget yourself
to
help
others,
and others
will
never
forget
you!

MEATS

"The life is more than meat, and the body is more than raiment."

Luke 12:23

Chicken Broccoli Casserole

Elaine Pyle, Franklin, N.C.

- 2 cups diced cooked chicken or turkey
- 1 10 oz. frozen broccoli stalks (cook in boiling water until barely tender)
- ½ tsp. salt
- 1 cup cheddar cheese, grated
- ½ cup mayonaise
- 2 tsps. lemon juice
- ¼ tsp. curry powder

Place chicken and broccoli in bottom of 1½ qt. casserole. Sprinkle with salt. Combine cheese, mayonaise, lemon juice, salt and curry powder and spread over top of chicken-broccoli mixture. Top with bread crumbs and dot with butter. This may be covered with plastic wrap and refrigerated until ready to use.

About 30 minutes before serving time, remove plastic wrap and bake in a moderate oven (350°) for about 30 minutes, or until bubbling hot.

Makes 4 servings

Chicken and Yellow Rice

Teresa Duke, Caryville, Fl.

4 lb. chicken
2/3 cup cooking oil
1 green pepper, chopped
1 onion, chopped
2 garlic cloves, chopped
2 large tomatoes
1 slice ham, 1/2 inch thick
4 cups boiling water
1 1/2 tsp. salt
1/8 tsp. pepper
1/2 tsp. saffron (you may substitute Tumeric)
3 cups rice
1/2 cup diced pimiento
1/2 cup sliced stuffed olives

Slowly brown chicken in oil, remove. Cook ham, onions and peppers 10 min. Add chicken and water. Bring to a boil, cover and simmer 35 min. Add salt, pepper and saffron. Cook 20 min. or until chicken is almost done. Add the rice and cook 30 min., stirring occasionally. Add pimiento, let stand 10 min., then place on a serving dish and garnish with olives.
Makes 6-8 servings

Chicken Wiggle

Zelma Frost, P.C.Fl.

1 large hen, boiled and cut into bite-size pieces
2 med. onions, chopped
2 bell peppers, chopped
1 jar pimentos, chopped
½ bottle worcestershire sauce
1 can english peas
1 lb. very small noodles
salt, pepper and garlic powder to taste

Cook onions and peppers in about a cup of chicken broth until tender. Boil noodles in broth. Mix all in a large baking dish. Bake slowly about 25 min at low temperature.

What God Hath Promised

God hath not promised
 skies always blue,
Flower strewn pathways
 all our lives through.
God hath not promised
 sun without rain,
Joy without sorrow,
 peace without pain.

But God hath promised
 strength for the day,
Rest for the laborer,
 light on the way;
Grace for the trial,
 help from above.
Unfailing sympathy,
 undying love.
          – copied –

"The Lord is not slack
concerning his promise"
          II Peter 3:9

Easy Oven Roast

Eloise Smith, P.C., Fl.

4 or 5 lb. Roast (any cut)
salt
½ - 1 Pkg. onion soup mix
Worcestershire sauce
Heinz 57 sauce
Catsup
3 or 4 medium potatoes (sliced)
3 or 4 medium carrots (sliced)
2 cups water

Line pan with foil large enough to make a tent around the ingredients. Place in lined pan, roast which has been salted all over. Pour Heinz 57, Worcestershire and Catsup over the roast. Cover the top with the dry onion soup mix. Place vegetables on top and around roast. Pour in the water. Pull foil over to make a tent.

Bake in 350° oven for 2½-3 hrs. or until tender. Thicken gravy if desired.

Chicken Parmesan

1   3 lb. frying chicken (cut up)
6 Tbsp. melted butter or margarine

Combine:

3 Tbsp. bread crumbs
½ cup grated parmesan cheese
dash of garlic salt
¼ cup chopped parsley

    Dip chicken pieces in butter. Butter a 9 X 13 inch baking dish. Add chicken pieces, sprinkle crumbs on top. Bake 1½ hours at 350°.

"Better is little with the fear of the Lord than great treasure and trouble therewith."
                    Proverbs 15:16

Crock Pot Steak

Lillie Martin   P.C., Fl.

1½ - 2 lbs. round steak (do not tenderize)
½ cup flour
1 green pepper
1 #2 can of tomatoes
1 pkg. frozen french style beans
3 tsp. soy sauce
3 tsp. molasses (syrup)

    Cut steak in serving pieces. Flour steak and brown in skillit in a small amount of oil.

    Put in crockpot, sprinkle a little flour over steak to thicken. Pour tomatoes, string beans, soy sauce and molasses over steak. Cut pepper in strips and add to mixture. Stir well.

    Cook 6 - 8 hours
Serve over rice   Very tasty!

"Be too busy to worry in the daytime, and you will be too tired to worry at night!"

Tasty Salmonettes

Louise Luker

1 - 15 oz. can pink salmon
1 whole egg
1 heaping tsp. baking powder
½ c. flour

    Drain juice from salmon, set aside. Put salmon in mixing bowl and stir in the egg. When it is gummy add ½ cup flour. Stir thoroughly. Mixture will be thick. Do not add any salt — pepper O.K.

    Take ¼ c. salmon juice (pour out excess) and add heaping tsp. of. B.P. to the juice and beat with a fork. It is going to foam. Fine! Measuring cup should be ¾ full. After foaming process, pour into salmon mixture. Mix again with fork. Drop by tsp. in hot oil. They will turn themselves over. Drain on paper towels.

Scalloped Oysters

1 pint oysters
¾ cup cream
2 tsps. worcestershire sauce
2 cups cracker crumbs
1 stick margarine
salt and pepper to taste

Melt margarine; add cracker crumbs, salt and pepper. Put ⅓ cracker mix in casserole and top with ½ oysters, the another ⅓ cracker mix and rest of oysters. Mix cream, oyster juice, worcestershire and pour over oysters. Top with remaining crumbs.

Bake at 350° for 40 min.

People may doubt what you say, but they will always believe what you do.

Chicken in a Stuffing Nest

Joan Twedell, Colo.

- 3 Tbsp. margarine
- 3 Tbsp. flour
- 1½ c. chicken broth
- ½ c. half & half
- 2 c. chicken
- 1 c. peas (cooked)
- ⅔ c. raw carrots (shredded)
- ½ c. onion (chopped)
- ¼ t. thyme
- ⅛ t. sage
- 1 stick oleo
- 1 c. boiling water
- 1 pkg. Stuffing mix

Melt butter. Add flour. Cook a few minutes. Gradually add broth. Cook until smooth and thick. Add cream, chicken, peas, carrots, onion, thyme, and sage. Prepare stuffing using 1 stick oleo and 1 c. boiling water. Press stuffing into casserole to make a nest. Pour hot mixture into center.

Bake at 400° about 15 min.

Impossible Tuna Pie

1 6½ oz. can of tuna (drained)
1 cup grated cheese
1 3 oz. pkg. cream cheese (cut up)
¼ cup sliced green onions
1 2 oz. jar chopped pimento (drained)
2 cups milk
1 cup Bisquick
4 eggs
¾ tsp salt

Mix tuna, cheeses, onions and pimento and put in 10x1½ inch pie plate (greased). Beat remaining ingredients 15 seconds in blender on high or 1 minute with hand beater. Pour into plate. Bake until knife inserted comes out clean.

Bake at 400° 35-40 min.

Swiss Steak Quickie

Dot the center of a 20-inch sheet of Heavy Duty Aluminum Foil with 1 tsp butter or margarine. Shake half the contents of 1 envelope onion soup mix on the foil. (dry)

Over this place 1½ lb. chuck or round steak, cut 1 inch thick. Top steak with remaining soup mix and 1 tsp. butter. Add ½ lb. fresh mushrooms, sliced, around steak. Bring foil up over meat and double-fold edges. Place in a shallow baking pan.

Bake 1 hour at 375°.

Children left to grow up like weeds are not likely to produce the flowers of genius.

Southern Chicken 'n Dressing

1 recipe corn bread
4 or 5 slices dry bread
4 hard-cooked eggs, diced
1 large onion, chopped
salt and pepper
2 beaten eggs
poultry seasoning
hot chicken broth
1 stewing chicken, cooked and boned

Combine all ingredients except chicken in large bowl, adding broth to moisten. Spread in greased casserole; press chicken pieces into dressing.

Bake in 400° oven 15-20 min.

"But the path of the just is as the shining light, that shineth more and more unto the perfect day."   Proverbs 4:18

A Mother Must:

Walk with God!
Put happiness in the home before greatness.
Not be the victim of her own disposition.
Make her tongue the law of kindness.
In discipline, be firm but patient.
Teach that right means behaving as well as believing.
Not only teach but live.
Not only speak but listen.
Realize that to lead her child to Christ is her highest privilege!

"The way to rise above others is to be glad when others rise above you!"

"Stuff"

Judy Clawson, Tx.

In electric skillet place 1-2 lbs. ground beef. Add layer of thinly sliced potatoes, layer of sliced carrots, and a layer of sliced onions. Top this with shredded cabbage. Add one can of cream of mushroom soup (chicken or celery). Do not stir. Cook on low heat for about 45 minutes.

This may be started with a higher temperature. When it bubbles be sure and turn it down or hamburger will burn.

"Thou shalt love thy neighbor as thyself."

Galatians 5:14

Chicken Casserole

Linda Crews   Sanford, Fl.

- 1 small chicken
- 1/4 lb. margarine (melted)
- 1 pkg. cornbread stuffing mix
- 1 can cream of Chicken soup
- or 1 can cream of Celery soup
- or 1 can cream of Onion soup

Cook chicken in salted water until tender, reserving broth. Take meat off the bones and arrange over bottom of casserole. Blend stuffing mix with melted margarine. In large bowl combine 2 cups broth with 2 cans soup. Cover chicken alternately with layers of stuffing and soup, allowing a small amount of stuffing to sprinkle over the top.

Heat in a moderate oven until hot enough to serve.
20-30 min.

Hamburger Stroganoff

Eunice Shafferman
Virginia

½ c. minced onion
¼ c. butter
1 lb. ground beef
2 Tbsp. flour
2 tsp. salt
¼ tsp. pepper
1 lb. fresh mushrooms
   or 8 oz. can.
10½ cream of chicken soup
   (undiluted)
1 cup sour cream
2 Tbsp. minced parsley

Sauté onion in butter over medium heat. Add meat and brown. Add flour, salt, pepper and mushrooms. Cook 5 min. Add soup, simmer uncovered 10 minutes.

Stir in sour cream. Heat through. Sprinkle with parsley. Serve over noodles.

4-6 servings

"Thou art my sister, and call understanding thy Kinswoman."
Proverbs 7:4

Savory Shrimp

Mrs. Chestnut, P.C., Fl.

3 tablespoons shortening
1 onion, chopped
1 green pepper, chopped
1 cup minced pimento
1 cup rice
1½ cups shrimp (cooked)
1 tsp. salt
1 bay leaf
2 cups tomato juice

Melt shortening, add all ingredients. Cover, when steam appears, turn off burner. Cook for 40 min. without removing cover.

A man of words and not of deeds is like a garden full of weeds.

Porcupine Meat Balls

1 lb. Ground Beef
½ c. raw rice
¼ c. chopped onion
1 tsp. salt
¼ tsp. pepper
16 oz. tomato sauce
1 cup water

    Mix beef, rice, onion, salt and pepper.
    Form into small balls. Fry in oil; brown on all sides. Add sauce, mix well.
    Cover and simmer for 45 min.

    After 40 life is mainly a maintenance job!

Marzetti

Serve 10-12

- 2 lb. ground beef
- 1 large stalk celery ⎫
- 1 large onion   ⎬ cut fine
- 1 green pepper   ⎭
- ½ lb. noodles
- 2 cans tomato soup
- ½ lb. sharp cheese

Fry meat in a little butter until slightly brown. Simmer veg. in a little water till almost done. Drop noodles in salted boiling water --- boil 3 min. Mix meat, veg., noodles, and tomato soup together and put in a casserole. Crumble cheese over top. Put in 350° oven, keep covered till cheese melts, uncover —

Bake 1 hour

This is one of my Mothers' recipes. I was surprised to see it in a recent "Good Housekeeping".

Others

Lord, help me live from day to day
   In such a self-forgetful way,
That even when I kneel to pray,
   My prayer shall be for others.

Help me in all the work I do
   to ever be sincere and true
And know, that all I do for you
   Must needs be done for others.

And when my work on earth is done,
   And my new work in Heaven's begun,
May I forget the crown I've won,
   While thinking still of others.

Others, Lord, yes, Others!
   Let this my motto be.
Help me to live for others
   That I may live for Thee.

          –copied–

Green Chilies Casserole

Louise Luker — Loop, Tx.

2 lbs. hamburger meat
1 can green chilies (chopped)
2 cans C. of Chicken soup plus
1 can water
1 pkg. tortillas
grated Amer. cheese
1 small onion
pepper, salt, and garlic to taste

Brown hamburger and onion. Add soup, garlic, salt, pepper and green chilies. Let simmer. In greased dish put layer of tortillas, add hamburger mixture, layer of cheese, until all ingredients are used. Bake at 350° 30 minutes

Chicken Corn Soup

(Pa. recipe — Donna Pyle)

4 lb. stewing hen
1 whole onion
4 qt. water
1 tbsp salt
2 cans corn
½ c. chopped celery
1 tbsp. chopped parsley

Ingredients for Rivels
1 cup flour
pinch salt
1 egg
milk

Cut chicken into pieces, and place in a large kettle with onion, water and salt. Bring to a boil over high heat, then lower heat to simmer. Cover and cook about 45 min. or until chicken is tender. When cool remove meat from the bones and cut into bite-size pieces. Return meat to the stock. Add corn and celery. Simmer 30 min.

To make Rivels:
Combine flour, salt, egg and enough milk to make a crumbly mixture with lumps the size of small peas. Drop rivels into the simmering soup and cook for 15 min. Add parsley, salt and pepper.

Shake and Bake for Chicken

Whip up your own from scratch — the equivalent of 20 packets — for ¼ the price! Just stir up:

- 4 cups flour
- 4 cups cracker meal
- 4 Tbsp. salt, 2 Tbsp. sugar,
- 2 tsp. each garlic and onion powder
- 3 tbsp. paprika
- ¼ cup oil

Store in refrigerator

"Don't brag about your children to your friends. If yours are smarter, your friends will be embarrassed and if theirs are smarter, they won't be impressed."

Company Chicken

8 boned chicken breasts
1 lb. jar chipped beef
8 strips bacon
1 can cream of mushroom soup

Cover bottom of 8 x 11 in. baking dish with the dried beef. Wrap one strip of bacon around each chicken breast and arrange over the beef slices.

Spread the undiluted soup over chicken.

Bake 2 hrs. at 300°

Increase oven temperature to 350° for another hour.

Baste several times during last hour.

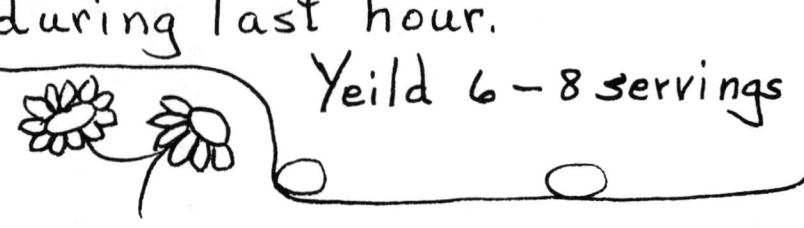

Yeild 6 - 8 servings

Chicken Every Sunday
Frances Marvin, N.Y.

8 chicken breasts or thighs (salted)
½ stick margarine
1 can cream of celery soup
1 can cream of mushroom soup
1 can cream of chicken soup
2 cans water
1½ cups uncooked rice

Dip chicken into melted margarine.

Mix soups and water.

Pour over rice in a casserole dish. Arrange chicken on top.

Cook uncovered at 250° for 2½ — 3 hours.

Turn higher the last 10 min. for browning.

Green Chili Enchiladas

Sheryl Myers — Carbondale, Colo.

1. Melt 4 Tbsp. butter in a saucepan.
2. Blend 6 Tbsp. flour.
3. Stir in 5 cups milk.
4. Cook over direct heat, stirring until thick.
5. Add: 2 tsp. salt, 1 c. grated amer. cheese, ½ - 1 cup chopped green chili, ½ clove garlic, minced.
6. Mix well, cover and let stand while frying tortillas.
7. Dip corn tortilla in small amount of hot oil, turning once (about 5 sec. on each side). Fry rest of tortillas in pkg. of 1 doz. Do not allow tortillas to become crisp.
8. Drain on absorbent paper.
9. Spread tortilla with small amount of cream sauce, finely chopped onion, and grated cheese.
10. Roll and arrange in shallow casserole.
11. Pour sauce over the 12 rolled enchiladas.

— continued —

12. Top each enchilada with grated cheese and place in oven at 350° for 8-10 minutes or until cheese is melted.
13. Garnish with shredded lettuce, ripe olives, and tomato wedges.

Serves 6-8

Golden Ham Pie
serves 6-8

Saute: 3 Tbsp. chopped onion and ¼ cup chopped green pepper in ¼ cup shortening.

Remove from heat and blend in: 6 Tbsp. flour, 2 c. milk, 1 can cr. of Chicken soup.

Bring to boil for 1 min., stirring constantly. Stir in 2 c. diced ham + 1 T. lemon juice. Pour into greased 8X12 baking dish and place in 450° oven while making cheese bisquits.

Mix: 1 c. flour, ½ t. salt, 1½ T. B.P. Stir in: 2½ T. shortening, ¾ c. grated cheese, 1 chopped pimento, + ⅓ c. milk. Knead lightly and roll out ¼" thick. Place on top of casserole and bake 15-20 min. longer.

Southern Fried Chicken

3 lb. frying chicken, cut up
1 egg, beaten
½ cup milk
flour
Salt and pepper
Cooking oil or shortening

Blend egg and milk. Dip chicken pieces into mixture, then roll in flour well seasoned with salt and pepper. Fry chicken in a heavy kettle, a few pieces at a time, in deep hot fat until golden brown and tender. Use a wire frying basket if available.

Keep pieces warm in 200° oven until all chicken is fried.

Serves 4

Stuffed Camel

Serves 200   from a Canadian Newspaper

1 whole med.-sized camel
20 whole med.-sized chickens
12 kilos rice
2 kilos almonds
110 Gal. water
Salt to taste
1 whole lamb
60 eggs
2 kilos pine nuts
1 kilo pistachio nuts
5 lb. pepper

Skin, clean and trim camel, lamb, and chickens. Boil all until tender. Cook rice until fluffy. Fry nuts until brown and mix with rice. Hard boil and peel eggs. Stuff the chickens with the egg-rice-nut mixture. Stuff the lamb with 5 chickens and more rice mixture. Stuff the camel with the lamb and more rice. Broil the stuffed camel in a large oven or near a flame until brown. Spread remaining rice mixture on a tray and place the camel on top. Place remaining cooked chickens around camel. Decorate with boiled eggs and nuts!

SALADS

Carrot and Orange Salad

Elaine Pyle, Franklin, N.C.

1 envelope unflavored gelatin
½ cup fresh or unsweetened orange juice
¼ cup sugar (or artificial sweetener)
1 cup water
3 Tbsp. lemon juice or vinegar
¼ tsp. salt
½ cup shredded raw carrots
½ cup canned unsweetened crushed pineapple (well-drained)
½ cup fresh orange sections (cut and drained)

Sprinkle gelatin in orange juice to soften. Add sweetener (or sugar). Place over low heat and stir until gelatine is dissolved. Remove from heat and add water, lemon juice (or vinegar) and salt. Chill until slightly firm. Makes 6 (½ cup) servings.

Apricot Jello Salad

Mary Jane Mattheis - Chatt. Tn.

2/3 cup water
1 large can crushed pineapple
8 oz. cream cheese
2 small jars apricot baby food
1 can Eagle brand milk
½ cup nuts
1 6 oz. box apricot jello

Bring water and pineapple juice to a boil — remove from heat — add pineapple, jello and baby food.

Soften cream cheese with milk and mix until smooth.

Mix milk and cheese with apricot mixture. Pour into 13 X 9 pan. Add nuts. Chill until firm.

Strawberry Jello Salad

Lucilla Hodges, P.C., Fl.

2 pkgs. strawberry jello
2 - 10 oz. pkgs. frozen strawberries (thawed)
2 cups crushed pineapple (undrained)
2 mashed bananas
1½ cups boiling water
1 cup sour cream

Mix jello and water, add strawberries, pineapple and bananas.

Pour half of mix into a shallow dish and let chill.

Pour sour cream over chilled jello and add other half of mix which has been at room temperature.

Refrigerate —

"If ye abide in me, and my words abide in you, ye shall ask what ye will, and it shall be done unto you."
John 15:7

Lunch Topic

The starving children of Bombay
came up at lunch the other day
again, when Tommy spurned his
spinach and squash - - -
    to even <u>touch</u>, less <u>finish</u>!
Some luscious liver-onion-covered,
long in its' casserole had hovered.

No plea of mine transformed his gleam
of horror for my gourmet "dream."
Then Tommy --- sure he'd saved the day,
yelled;
    "Mom, lets' ship it to Bombay!"

                   Ruth W. Shively - Texas
                      (my sister)

Esthers' Potato Salad

6 cups boiled potatoes
1 cup finely chopped celery
1 small minced onion
3 or 4 hard cooked eggs (chopped)
¼ cup cubed pickles (optional)
Kraft Real Mayonaise

Boil potatoes (I allow about 1 potato for each serving) and let them cool thoroughly. Cube the potatoes and lightly toss in the celery, onions, eggs, and pickles.

Mix with enough mayonaise to hold together well.

"The one hopeless person is he, Who thinks he's already good enough!"

Southern Magnolia

How to Cook a Husband

A good many husbands are utterly spoiled by mismanagement in cooking and so are not tender and good. Some women keep them constantly in hot water; others let them freeze by their carelessness and indifference. Some keep them in a stew with irritating ways and words. Some wives keep them pickled, while others waste them shamefully.

It cannot be supposed that any husband will be tender and good so managed, but he will be really delicious when properly prepared.

In selecting a husband, you should be guided not by silvery appearance as you would in buying a mackerel, nor by the golden tint as you would in buying salmon. Do not go to the market for him, as the best ones are always brought to the door. Be sure to select him yourself, as tastes differ.

It is far better not to have one at all unless you will patiently learn how to cook him.

Of course, a preserving kettle of the finest porcelain is best, but if you have nothing better than an earthenware pipkin, it will do. Like crabs and lobsters, husbands are cooked alive. They sometimes fly out of the kettle and so become burned and crusty on the edges, so it is wise to secure them in the kettle with a silken cord called <u>comfort</u> as the one called <u>duty</u> is apt to be weak.

Make a clear, steady flame of <u>Love</u>, <u>Warmth</u>, and <u>Cheerfulness</u>, and set him as near this as seems to agree with him. If he sputters do not be anxious, for some husbands do this until they are quite done. Add a little sugar in the form of <u>Kisses</u>, but use no pepper or vinegar on any account. Season to taste with the spices <u>good humor</u> and <u>gaiety</u>. Avoid sharpness in testing him for tenderness. Stir him gently, lest he lie too flat and close to the kettle and so become useless.

You cannot fail to know when he is done. If so treated, you will find him very digestible, agreeing with you perfectly; and he will keep as long as you choose unless you become careless and allow the home fires to grow cold.

Thus prepared, he will serve a lifetime of happiness.

— Copied from an 1800 cookbook —

"Who can find a virtuous woman? for her price is far above rubies.

The heart of her husband doth safely trust in her, so that he shall have no need of spoil.

She will do him good and not evil all the days of her life.

She seeketh wool, and flax, and worketh willingly with her hands."

Proverbs 31:10-13

Shrimp Salad

Lucilla Hodges, P.C. Fl.

1 head of lettuce, chopped
3 cups boiled shrimp
1½ cups celery, chopped
6 hard-boiled eggs, chopped
4½ tsp. lemon juice
Salt and pepper to taste
¾ cup mayonaise

Mix all ingredients lightly. Serve on crisp lettuce.

"It is of the Lord's mercies that we are not consumed, because his compassions fail not.

They are new every morning; great is thy faithfulness."

Lamentations 3: 22 + 23

Lemon Jello Salad

Jackie Pyle Atlanta, Ga.

1 Package lemon jello
1 small pkg. cream cheese
2 medium carrots (grated)
½ cup chopped celery
¼ cup chopped nuts
½ cup crushed pineapple

Mix jello according to the directions using a little less water. Add softened cream cheese then vegetables and top with the nuts.

Chill until firm and serve on a lettuce leaf.

Burdens

Bear own – – – – – Galatians 6:5
Bear one anothers' – – Galatians 6:2
Cast on the Lord – – Psalms 55:22

Lemon Blueberry Salad

Nell Helms, Al.

1 package lemon jello (3 oz.)
1 package black rasberry jello (3 oz.)
1 cup. boiling water
½ cup cold water
1 Tbsp. lemon juice
1 21 oz. can blueberry pie filling
¼ cup sifted confectioners sugar
1 cup sour cream

   Make jello; gradually stir in pie filling. Pour in 8 x 8 x 12 inch baking dish. Chill till firm. Fold sugar into sour cream and spread over jello.

"There is that maketh himself rich, yet hath nothing: there is that maketh himself poor, yet hath great riches."
                    Proverbs 13:7

Fruit Salad

Joyce Casey, Festus, Mo.

1 can fruit cocktail
1 can crushed pineapple
1 cup small marshmallows
6 ripe bananas
6 or 8 maraschino cherries

Add and stir in one box of banana cream instant pudding.

Pink Cloud Fruit Salad Dressing

½ cup plain yogurt
½ cup strawberry yogurt
1½ tsp. lemon juice
dash of salt

or, try one my pastors' wife, Betty Ker, makes:

use half fruit-flavored yogurt and half cool whip.

Delicious as a dip for fruit!

Tuna Fish Salad

1 or 2 cans tuna
1 cup spaghetti (break up)
   (cook in salted water 7-10 min., drain)
1 cup celery
2 or 3 boiled eggs
1 can shredded pimento
½ cup diced sweet pickles
½ cup diced green peppers
½ cup olives
juice of 1 lemon
½ cup diced onion
   Add enough mayonaise to moisten and mix.

To prevent spaghetti or macaroni from boiling over add a pat of butter or a little veg. oil. This also keeps pasta from sticking together.

Chicken Salad

1 Chicken
1 cup pecans (chopped)
1 can crushed pineapple with juice
2 stalks celery (chopped)
1 large apple (diced)

Cook chicken in small amount of water until tender. Cool, and remove meat from the bones. Cut chicken in small pieces.

Add all the other ingredients and enough mayonaise to moisten.

Serve on lettuce leaves.

This is a favorite family recipe that we collected in Georgia many years ago.

O bless my little kitchen, Lord,
and those who enter in;
May they find naught but joy and peace
And happiness therein.

Three Bean Salad

Sally H.   Troy, O.

1 – 1 lb. can cut green beans
1 – 1 lb. can wax beans
1 – 1 lb. can kidney beans
½ cup chopped green pepper
½ cup chopped onions
½ cup vinegar
¾ cup. sugar
1 tsp. salt
1 tsp. celery seed

Combine all ingredients. Make the day before using.

"A lady is a woman who makes it easy for a man to be a gentleman!"

~~~~~~~~~~

"Think how smart we'd all be if we retained as much of what we read as we do of what we eat."

Growing in God's Garden
by Judy Hess

Lettuce: Love
Listen
Encourage

Beet: Anger
Self
Depression

Squash: Gossip
Lies
Negativism

Turnip: Smiling
Content
Faithful

Make Ahead Vegetable Salad
Virginia — Eunice S.

½ to 1 head lettuce - chopped or shredded
1 cup celery - sliced thin
½ cup green pepper - chopped
1 can water chestnuts - sliced thin
½ to 1 onion - chopped small
1½ cups grated cheddar cheese
6 eggs, hardcooked, chopped
bacos or crumbled bacon (6 slices)
one 10-oz pkg. frozen peas (unthawed)
1½ cups mayonaise (room temp.)
2 tbsp. sugar (or less)

Put ingredients in layers in large glass salad bowl in order listed with peas on top. Cover with mayonaise and sugar mixture. Chill from 12-24 hours. Either toss before serving or let people spoon down through layers as they serve themselves.

Salad Supreme

Jean H.   Troy, O.

Step I:
2 small or 1 lg. box Orange jello
1 #2 can crushed pinapple
(save the juice)

Mix jello according to directions and pour into 8x12 in. dish. Allow to almost congeal, then add pinapple. Sprinkle chopped nuts over jello and return to refrigerator. Let this congeal.

Step II:
Whip 1 lg. box Dream Whip. Blend one 8 oz. pkg. cream cheese (softened) with Dream Whip. Spread this over congealed jello. Cover dish and return to Refrig.

Step III:
Mix 1 cup pinapple juice, 1 Tbsp. lemon juice, ¾ c. sugar, 2 Tbsp. plain flour, and 2 well-beaten eggs. Cook until thick. When cool spread over step II. Sprinkle with nuts.

note: mix all of step III before heating to cook.

"It is better to have your bank account in heaven than to have your heaven in a bank"

Taco Salad

1 large head lettuce
   Break into bowl.
Add:
   4 tomatoes (cut up)
   1 large onion (diced)
   1 bag taco flavored chips (crushed)
   ½ lb. grated cheese
   1 8 oz. bottle catalina dressing

Brown 1 lb. ground beef and drain. Add 1 can chili beans and simmer 10 min. Pour over lettuce mixture and toss.

We lose on what ourselves we spend,
We have as treasures without end,
Whatever, Lord to thee we lend
   Who givest all.

Whatever, Lord, we lend to Thee,
Repaid a thousand-fold will be;
Then gladly will we give to Thee
   Who givest all.
   — Author unknown —

Freezer Coleslaw

Eleanor Guisewhite
Pa.

2 heads cabbage, shredded
1 lg. stalk celery, diced
1 lg. green or red pepper, diced
1 Tbsp. salt

Combine all ingredients in a bowl and mix. Set bowl in a large pan filled with cracked ice, for 1 hour.

Boil together the following for 15 min. and let cool:

2 c. vinegar
1 c. water
4 c. sugar
2 tsp. celery seed
2 tsp. mustard seed

When cabbage mixture is chilled and liquid is cooled, pour into containers and freeze.

How to Preserve Children

Take:

- 1 large grassy field
- ½ dozen children
- 2 or 3 small dogs
- a pinch of brook
- some small pebbles

Mix the children and dogs well together and put them in the field, stirring constantly. Pour the brook over the pebbles, sprinkle the field with flowers, spread over all a deep blue sky, and bake in a hot sun. When thoroughly browned, remove and set to cool in a bathtub!

— Author unknown

Conch Salad
Donna Pyle — Nassau, Bahamas

4 medium Conch (diced)
1 medium onion (chopped)
1 medium sweet pepper (diced)
1 or 2 stalks celery (chopped)
1 tsp. salt
hot pepper (optional)
6 or 8 sour oranges, lemons, or limes

Mash peppers in juice with salt. Pour over other chopped ingredients. Best if allowed to stand for 30 minutes.

Carrot and Raisin salad

Grate as many carrots as desired, add sugar, raisins and nuts.

Mix with mayonaise.

Sweet Sour Bean Salad

- 1 can green beans
- 1 can kidney beans
- 1 can yellow beans
- 1 red sweet onion, sliced
- 1 cup celery, chopped
- 1 small green pepper, chopped

Dressing

- ½ cup sugar
- ½ tsp. pepper
- 1 tsp. salt
- ¼ c. salad oil
- ⅔ c. vinegar

Drain and put into large bowl 3 types of beans. Then add pepper, onion, and celery. Mix ingredients for dressing, shake well, and pour over salad. Toss and put in refrigerator to marinate overnight.

Cranberry Salad

1 cup cranberries, ground
1 cup sugar
1 cup chopped pecans
½ cup celery, chopped fine
1 9 oz. can crushed pineapple
juice of 1 lemon
2 cups boiling water
1 pkg. strawberry or lemon jello

    Mix sugar and cranberries together and let stand overnight or for several hours. Add jello to boiling water and stir until dissolved. Add other ingredients and chill. Substitute the juice from the pineapple for some of the water, if desired.

VEGETABLES

Turnip Greens

Greens are best when young and tender. Select those which are crisp, tender and have a bright color. Allow about 2 lbs. of greens to serve 4. Wash greens several times and break off any tough stems. Put bacon grease or cooking oil in a large pot with the greens. Bring to a boil, reduce heat, and simmer for about one hour. Add salt and pepper. The water that clings to the greens after washing them may be enough liquid. If not add a little more. Using a sharp knife chop the greens before serving.

"Every wise woman buildeth her house; but the foolish plucketh it down with her hands."

Proverbs 14:1

Southern Fried Corn

Cut the kernals from 10 or 12 ears of corn. I use a special corn cutter that grates it off. Scrape the ears to get all of the juice.

Heat a large iron skillet and add a small amount of bacon grease or cooking oil.

Pour in the corn and cook quickly, stirring constantly. Add water as need to keep at right consistency. Turn fire down and simmer a few min.

I learned to cook corn this way from my neighbor, Thelma, when we once lived in Atlanta, Ga.

Sweet Potato Casserole

3 cups mashed, cooked, sweet potatoes
1 cup sugar
½ cup milk
⅓ cup butter
2 eggs
1 tsp. vanilla

    Combine above ingredients in a shallow baking dish.

Topping:
1 cup coconut
1 cup chopped pecans
1 cup brown sugar
⅓ cup flour
⅓ cup melted butter

    Mix above ingredients well and sprinkle over sweet potatoes.

    Bake at 350° until brown.

Green Rice

2 cups cooked rice
1 pkg. chopped broccoli
1 chopped onion
½ lb. cubed cheese
2 beaten eggs
½ cup corn oil
1 cup milk
Salt and pepper to taste

Prepare broccoli as directed on package. Mix all ingredients together and pour into a greased baking dish.
Bake 1 hour at 350°

Serves 10-12

"Give, and it shall be given unto you; good measure, pressed down, and shaken together, and running over, shall men give into your bosom."
Luke 6:38

Company Potatoes
Joan Twedell, Colo.

1 pint sour cream
10 oz. (2 cups) grated sharp cheese
2 lb. frozen hash browns
½ cup melted butter
1 tsp. salt
½ tsp. pepper
½ cup chopped onions
1 can cream of chicken soup

    Defrost hash browns. Mix all the above ingredients together and put into a buttered 3-quart casserole dish.

    Mix ¼ cup melted butter with 2 cups of crushed corn flakes and sprinkle on top of potato mixture. Cover casserole and bake at 350° for about 45 minutes or til bubbly.

    Serves 10-12

Things Christians Ought to do.

Tithe
Matt. 23:23

Worship
John 4:20

Obey
Acts 5:29

Pray
Rom. 8:26

Teach
Heb. 5:12

Be Holy
II Peter 3:11

Bear Burdens
Rom. 15:1

H.F. Pyle

Broccoli Casserole

Joan Twedell
Colo.

2 pkg. frozen broccoli (cooked)
2 cups rice (cooked)
1 8 oz. jar cheese spread or 3 slices american cheese
1 cup chopped celery
½ cup milk
¼ cup butter
1 chopped onion
1 can cream of chicken soup
Salt and pepper

Place broccoli and rice in a 2 quart casserole. Stir in half of the cheese. Melt butter in a skillet. Add onion and celery and cook until tender. Stir in soup and milk. Season to taste. Pour over other mixture and mix well. Top casserole with rest of cheese and bake 30 min. at 350°.

Fried Okra

This is my son David's favorite vegetable. Grandmom Pyle taught me how to fry it for him.

Wash and dry the okra. Cut off the stem ends and tips. Cut the okra pods into 1/4 inch slices.

Combine salt with enough corn meal to mix with the okra or use self-rising mix. Put the corn meal in a paper bag and add the okra and shake until the okra is coated.

Fry in shallow fat until brown on all sides. Do not have fire too hot. Drain on paper towels.

David's wife, Donna, now takes care of this job!

Rice Casserole

Colleen Dickens — Panama City

1 cup rice
6 cups water
1 tsp. salt

Boil 20-25 minutes

Simmer in ½ stick butter for 10 minutes:

1 onion (chopped)
1 stalk celery (chopped)

Drain and rinse rice.

Add: onion and celery
1 bottle olives (sliced)
1 can evaporated milk

Stir good.

Bake 1 hour and 30 minutes at 350°

Faith makes all things possible;
Hope makes all things bright;
Love makes all things easy.

Broccoli Casserole

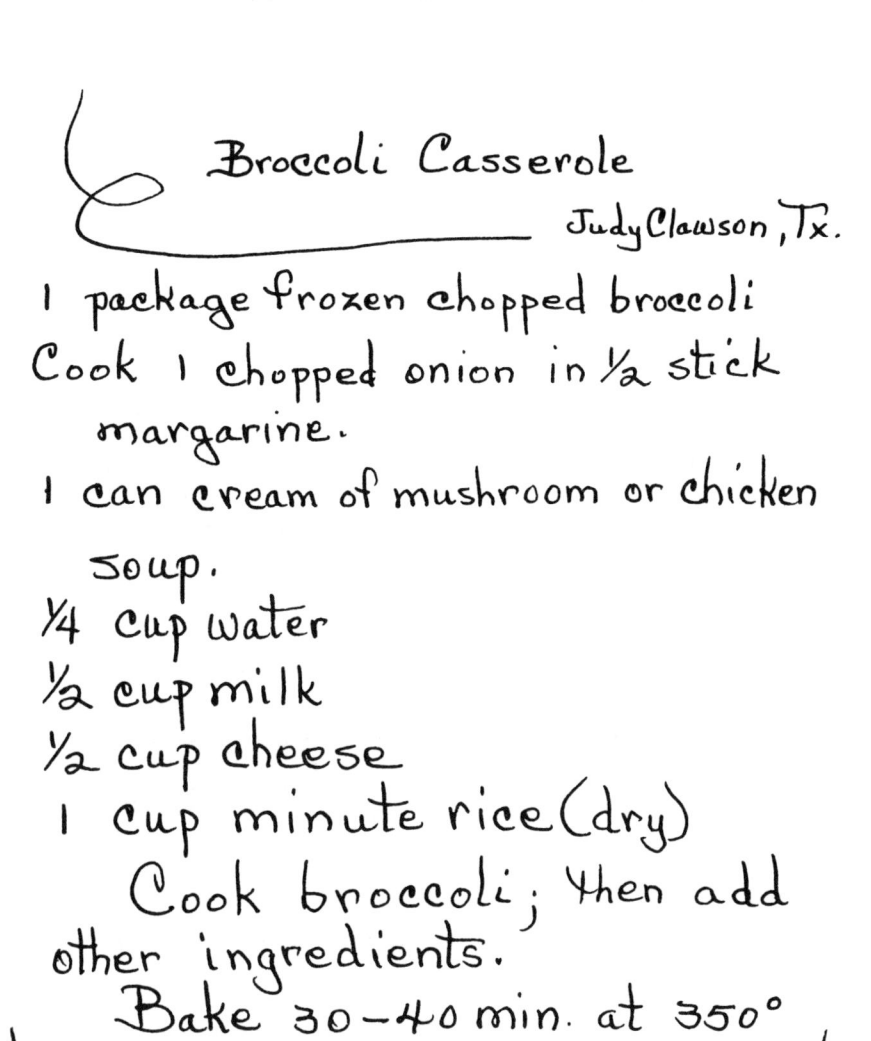

— Judy Clawson, Tx.

1 package frozen chopped broccoli

Cook 1 chopped onion in ½ stick margarine.

1 can cream of mushroom or chicken soup.

¼ cup water

½ cup milk

½ cup cheese

1 cup minute rice (dry)

Cook broccoli; then add other ingredients.

Bake 30-40 min. at 350°

"Bear ye one another's burdens, and so fulfil the law of Christ."

Galatians 6:2

A Touch of Red

by Ruth W. Shively
(my sister)

"Every room needs a touch of red"--
this is what my sister said.
So I bought cherry vases, dishes,
against my irate spouse's wishes;
sprayed one lampshade crimson bright
(it really makes a lovely light);
the sofa, dully-green and worn,
in gay vermillion was reborn.
We threw a party, dozens came,
Christmas candles lit our game;
with scarlet ribbons in my wig,
I thought our bash was very big.
Then someone splashed cranberry punch
On white lace I had spread for lunch,
And my poor husband's boss's wife
cut herself with a ruby knife!

But at least I had a touch of red
in every room, like sister said!

Beets and Pineapple

Ruth Shively — Irving, Texas

1 Jar - ready-to-heat Harvard beets (approx. 1 lb.)
1 can pineapple tidbits (13½ oz. size)

Drain off most of the juice from the pineapple; then combine the beets and pineapple in a saucepan and stir occasionally till heated. This will serve 5 or 6.

"The fear of the Lord is the beginning of wisdom: and the knowledge of the holy is understanding."   Proverbs 9:10

Eggplant Casserole

1 medium eggplant
2 slices bacon, diced
1 medium onion, chopped
1 medium potato, grated
1 can mushroom soup, undiluted
½ cup ritz crackers

Peel eggplant, and cut into 1 inch cubes; cook in small amount of water 10 min. Drain well.

Fry bacon until crisp. Stir in onion and potato; cook until onion is tender. Add eggplant and soup, stirring well.

Spoon into greased 1½ quart baking dish. Sprinkle with the cracker crumbs.

Bake at 350° for 30 minutes.

6 servings

Peas and Rice
a favorite Bahamian Recipe

1/4 lb. butter
1/4 lb. bacon
3 med onions
1 stalk celery
5 oz. tomato paste
2 fresh tomatoes
1/2 pint peas (pigeon or blackeye)
3 cups rice
4/5 qt. water
thyme
salt and pepper

Put butter and bacon in saucepan and cook bacon until crisp, add onions and celery until soft, then add tomato paste and fresh tomatoes. Cook for 15 min.
Add peas, water, rice and seasoning.
Cover saucepan and bring to a boil.
Reduce heat and cook for about 45 min.

J. Albury
Nassau,
Bahamas

Macaroni and Cheese

Jeanni Albury, Nassau

1 8 oz. box macaroni
1 lb. cheese
3/4 cup butter
2 cans evaporated milk
2 eggs
1 small onion (optional) chopped
Salt to taste

Cook macaroni and drain. Add butter then cheese until cheese is a little melted. Next add milk and eggs and onion. Mix well and bake in a greased casserole until golden brown.

This is one of the recipes I collected in the Bahamas while we were there in a revival meeting. Our son and his wife taught in a Christian school there for 4 years.

Potato Casserole

Eunice S., Va.

- 1 Package frozen hash brown potatoes (24-32 oz. size)
- 1 can c. of potato soup
- 1 can c. of celery soup
- ½ cup chopped green pepper
- ½ cup chopped onion
- 8 oz. sour cream
- ⅓ - ½ cup milk

Mix frozen hash browns, green pepper, and onion. Put in a greased baking dish. Pour soups, milk, and sour cream over potatoes. Bake at 350° for 2½ hrs.

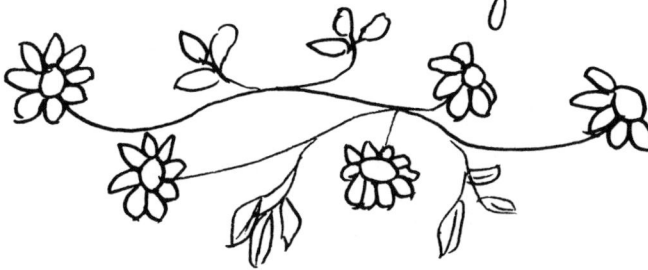

Squash Souffle

Sherrill Bondeson — P.C., Fla.

1 lb. squash
1 large onion } cook together; drain and mash.

1 cup grated cheese
¼ cup butter
3 egg yolks
½ cup milk
8-10 crackers (crumbled)
salt and pepper to taste

Add to squash.

Beat 3 egg whites until stiff, and fold in.

Bake in a buttered mold or casserole until lightly brown and firm.

350° — 40 minutes

"She looketh well to the ways of her household, and eateth not the bread of idleness."

Proverbs 31:27

Rutabagas and Apples

Rhea Holloway — Clarksville, Ga.

3 cups cooked and mashed rutabagas
1 ½ cups canned apple slices
¼ cup brown sugar
1 cup flour
1 stick softened margarine
⅓ cup sugar

Mix first three ingredients together and put in casserole dish. With pastry cutter mix remaining ingredients together till crumbly. Spread on top of rutabaga mixture. Bake at 350° until heated through and crust is brown.

Yeild — 8 servings

Quick Creamed Spinach

Eunice Shafferman (my sister) — Va.

1 pkg. frozen chopped spinach
1 ½ Tbsp. butter
½ tsp. salt
Dash of accent
½ tsp. onion powder
1 Tbsp. flour
½ cup sour cream

Partially thaw spinach. In heavy pan melt butter, add spinach and seasonings.

Cook, covered, over high heat 1 or 2 minutes; lower heat, cook 5 minutes longer, breaking up with fork to hasten thawing. Sprinkle flour over spinach, blend well. Add sour cream, blend, cook over low heat about 2 minutes.

Serves 4

Hash Brown Potato Casserole

1 (2 lb. pkg) frozen hash-brown potatoes
½ cup melted margarine
1 tsp. salt
¼ tsp pepper
½ cup chopped onion
1 can cream of mushroom soup
1 pint sour cream
2 cups grated mild cheddar cheese
2 cups corn flakes
¼ cup melted margarine

Mix together potatoes, ½ cup margarine, salt, pepper, onion, soup, sour cream and cheese.

Place in 9 X 13-inch casserole. Combine corn flakes and ¼ cup melted margarine and sprinkle over other ingredients.

Bake 45 min. at 350°

"A soft answer turneth away wrath."   Proverbs 15:1

"But seek ye first the Kingdom of God, and His righteousness, and all these things shall be added unto you."

Matthew 6:33

Asparagus Casserole

Iris Sowell, P.C., Fl.

- 2 large cans asparagus spears
- 1 cup chopped nuts
- 1 stick oleo
- 1 stack crackers
- 1½ cups Velveeta (small box)

Heat liquid, add oleo. Mix 1 cup water and 2 tbsps. flour. Pour slowly into boiling mixture. Stir — add cheese and melt. Make 3 layers of asparagus, crackers and nuts.
Pour sauce over all.
Sprinkle crackers and nuts on top.
Bake at 475° until brown about 5 minutes.

Shoe Peg Corn Casserole

Barbara Dawkins, P.C., Fl.

½ cup chopped onion
1 cup chopped celery
½ c. chopped green pepper
1 c. grated cheese
1 can whole kernel corn
1 can string beans
or 2 cans corn

1 can c. of celery soup
1 cup sour cream
salt
pepper
1 stick oleo
1 stack ritz crackers

Mix all ingredients except crackers and oleo. Stir and pour in greased 9 X 13 baking dish. Melt oleo and crunch crackers and mix together. Sprinkle over top of casserole.
Bake about 30 minutes in 350° oven.

"And ye now therefore have sorrow: but I will see you again, and your heart shall rejoice, and your joy no man taketh from you."
John 16:22

Butterbeans, Peas and Okra

This is a combination of vegetables that I learned to cook when we moved to North Florida. It is a favorite here and in southern Alabama where there are plenty of these delicious vegetables in the early summer.

Use about equal amounts of fresh butterbeans and white-acre peas.

Boil with enough water to partly cover.

Lay a few pods of okra on top for flavor. Also use a little bacon grease for flavor.

"Ask, and ye shall receive, that your joy may be full."
—John 16:24-b

Panama City Beach, Fl.

DESSERTS

Buttermilk Pie

Adnie Thomas, P.C., Fla.

1 1/3 cups sugar
1/2 cup butter
3 Tbsp. self-rising flour
2 eggs
1 cup buttermilk
1 tsp. vanilla

Cream butter and sugar. Add eggs and flour and mix well. Add vanilla and buttermilk last. Bake in unbaked pie shell 35-45 minutes in a 350° oven.

"Her children arise up, and call her blessed."
                    Proverbs 31:28a

Downtowner Fudge Pie

Iris Arnold, Orlando

In top of double-boiler or over low heat melt:
- ½ cup (1 stick) butter
- 3 sq. unsweetened chocolate

Meanwhile, place in mixing bowl and beat until light:
- 4 eggs

Beat into the eggs:
- 3 Tbsp. white karo
- 1½ cup sugar
- ¼ tsp. salt
- 1 tsp. vanilla

Now add the choc. mix, (slightly cooled) mix thoroughly and pour into a pie shell. Bake at 350° for 25-30 min. or until top is crusty and filling is set but still somewhat soft inside. Do not overbake. Pie should shake like custard so it will not be too stiff when cool.

Serve plain or with ice cream.

Instant Pumpkin Pie

- 1 envelope Dream whip
- 1 6 serving size vanilla instant pudding
- 1 16 oz. can pumpkin
- 1 cup milk
- ½ tsp. nutmeg
- ½ tsp. ginger
- ½ tsp. cinnamon
- 1 baked 9 inch pie shell, cooled

Prepare whipped topping mix as directed on pkg. Combine 1 cup of the prepared topping with the pie filling mix, pumpkin, milk, and spices. Mix slowly with rotary beater just until blended, about 1 minute. Pour into pie shell. Chill until set, at least 2 hours.

Garnish with remaining topping.

Jam Squares

Nell Helms, Al.

1 cup flour
½ tsp. Baking soda
½ tsp. salt
2 cups oatmeal
¾ cup brown sugar (sifted)
¾ cup margarine
½ pint fruit preserves

Mix dry ingredients. Mix in oats and sugar. Cut in butter and turn 2 cups into a buttered pan. Pat down evenly. Spread with preserves. Sprinkle remaining flour mix over preserves. Pat down lightly.

Bake 25 min. in 350° oven.

"A merry heart doeth good like a medicine: but a broken spirit drieth the bones."
Proverbs 17:22

Holiday Fruit Cookies

Ann Pyle, Ellenwood, Ga.

1 cup soft shortening
2 cups brown sugar (packed)
2 eggs
½ cup buttermilk, water, or sour milk
3½ cups sifted self-rising flour
1½ cups pecans
2 cups dates (cut up)
2 cups cherries or other candied fruit (cut up)

Mix thoroughly shortening, brown sugar and eggs. Stir in buttermilk and flour. Mix in pecans, dates and candied fruit. Chill at least 1 hr. Heat oven to 400°. Drop by rounded teaspoonfuls about 2" apart on a lightly greased baking sheet.

Bake 8–10 minutes until almost no imprint remains when lightly touched.

Makes 8 dozen cookies.

Cheese Ball

Ann Pyle, Ellenwood, Ga.

14 ozs. cream cheese
½ cup sour cream
8 ozs. pineapple (drained)
4 ozs. chopped cherries
1 Tbsp. chopped onion
1 Tbsp. seasoned salt
2 cups chopped pecans

Roll in ½ cup chopped pecans.

"Thy word is a lamp unto my feet,
and a light unto my path."

Psalms 119:105

Molasses Cookies

Makes 3 Dozen

1 cup sugar
1 cup shortening
1 cup molasses
1 egg
2 tsp. soda (dissolve in 5 Tbsp. cold water)
1 tsp. salt
1 tsp. cinnamon
1 tsp. ginger
4½ cups flour

Mix and place in refrigerator for a while, then roll and cut. Bake at 375°—

These were served for breakfast on the farm where we used to visit our Aunt and cousins when we were children.

Fruit Pizza
Barbara Hendricks

1 Pkg. refrig. sugar cookie dough
8 oz. pkg. cream cheese
⅓ cup sugar
½ tsp. Vanilla

Cut dough into ⅛ in. slices. Line 14 in. greased pizza pan with slices.

Bake at 375° for 12 min. or until lightly browned. Cool.

Blend softened cream cheese, sugar and vanilla.

Spread over cookie crust.

Top with banana slices, blueberries, strawberries or any favorite fruit.

Apple Slices

Marilyn Charles — Grampian, Pa.

2½ cups flour
1 Tbsp. sugar
1 tsp salt
1 cup crisco
1 egg separated
milk

⅔ c. crushed corn flakes
5 cups sliced peeled apples
1½ cups sugar
1 tsp. cinnamon

Glaze: 1 c. confectioners sugar
1 Tbsp. lemon juice

Sift together flour, sugar, and salt. Cut in crisco. Put egg yolk into cup and add milk to make ⅔ cup. Add to crisco mixture and mix enough to gather into a ball. Roll out half of dough to 11×15 in rectangle. Transfer to baking sheet. Cover with flakes and apple slices. Mix sugar and cinnamon, sprinkle over apples. Roll out other half of dough for top. Place over apples. Pinch edges together. Beat egg whites until stiff. Spread on top. Bake 40 min. at 400°.
While hot spread glaze over top.
Cut in 16 squares.

Chocolate Peanut Butter Dessert

Marilyn Charles   Gronpian, Pa.

Layer 1

3/4 c. crushed dry roasted peanuts
1 c. flour
1/2 c. butter

    Mix well and pat in bottom of 13×9 ungreased pan and bake for 20 min. at 350°. Cool

Layer 2

1/4 c. Peanut butter
8 oz. cream cheese
1 c. confectioners sugar
8 oz. cool whip

    Combine ~ mix well and spread over layer 1.

Layer 3

1 3 oz. pkg. choc. instant pudding
1 3 oz. pkg. vanilla instant pudding
2 3/4 c. milk

    Mix and spread over layer 2.

Layer 4

8 oz. container cool whip
    Spread over Layer 3

Fairy Pie

Lillie Martin   P.C., Fla.

½ cup butter
¼ cup sugar
4 egg yolks
¼ cup milk

⅔ cup flour
¼ tsp. salt
1 tsp. Baking Powder

Cream butter, add sugar gradually, Add egg yolks one at a time, Beat well after each addition. Add dry ingredients alternately with the milk. Pour into 8 inch cake pans. Cover with meringue made as follows:

4 egg whites
1 cup sugar
1 tsp. salt

¼ tsp. vanilla
¼ cup chopped nuts

Add salt to egg whites and beat until stiff, add sugar gradually, then add vanilla. Pile the meringue on cake batter, putting half on each layer, put on nut meats, Bake 25 min. at 325°. When cool place one layer on large cake plate, Cover with whipped cream. Put other layer on top, meringue side up.

Blackberry Cobbler

Berdie Vandiver — Sautee, Ga.

1 Pint blackberries
Sugar to taste
pie crust

Put a layer of berries in the bottom of a pan, sprinkle with sugar and dot with butter. Add thin strips of crust and repeat 'till all berries are used.

Cook on top of the stove over low heat for a few minutes until it boils good.

Put in a moderate oven until the top crust is brown.

Banana Split Pie

Carole Ross, Ohio

2 cups graham crackers (crushed)
3 sticks margarine
2 cups confectioners sugar
2 eggs
½ cup chopped nuts
4 bananas (sliced crosswise)
1 #2 can crushed pineapple (drained)
1 large carton cool-whip

Melt 1 stick margarine and mix with cracker crumbs. Spread evenly on bottom of large pan. Combine eggs, 2 sticks margarine, and sugar. Beat 15 min. Spoon over crumbs and arrange sliced bananas over it. Spred drained pineapple over bananas. Spread cool-whip over the top and sprinkle with nuts. Put cherries on top.

Serves 10-12

Lemon Cheese Bars

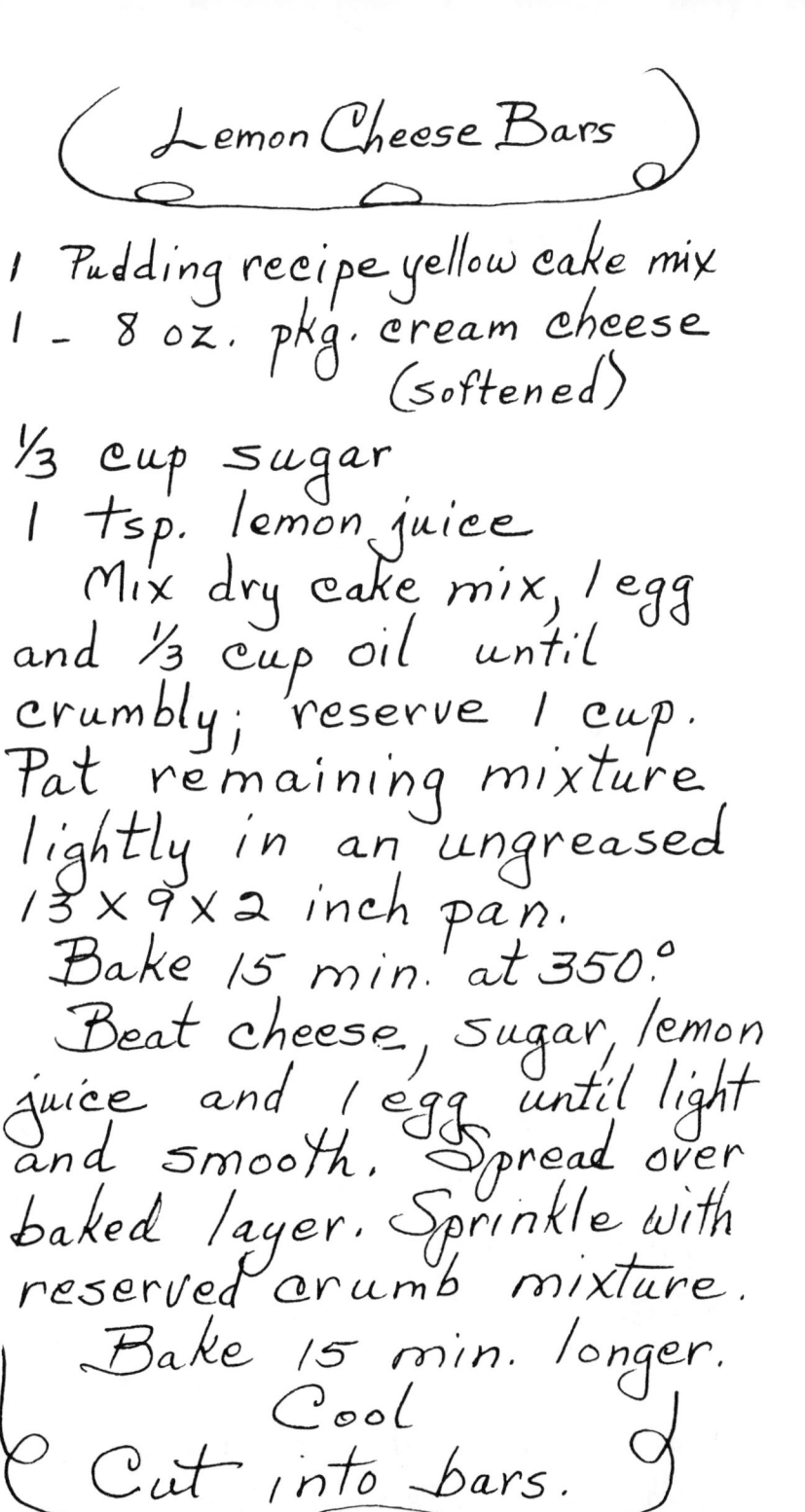

1 Pudding recipe yellow cake mix
1 - 8 oz. pkg. cream cheese (softened)
1/3 cup sugar
1 tsp. lemon juice

Mix dry cake mix, 1 egg and 1/3 cup oil until crumbly; reserve 1 cup. Pat remaining mixture lightly in an ungreased 13 x 9 x 2 inch pan.

Bake 15 min. at 350°.

Beat cheese, sugar, lemon juice and 1 egg until light and smooth. Spread over baked layer. Sprinkle with reserved crumb mixture.

Bake 15 min. longer.
Cool
Cut into bars.

Angel Pie

Faye Skipper, Ohio

- 4 tbsp. corn starch
- 3/4 cup sugar
- 1 1/2 cup boiling water
- 1 1/2 tsp. vanilla
- 3/8 tsp salt
- 3 egg whites
- 3 tbsp. sugar
- 1/2 cup whipped cream
- broken nuts

Mix corn starch and sugar in a saucepan. Add boiling water, stirring constantly. Cook until thick and clear; 10-12 minutes. Add salt to egg whites and beat until stiff. Add 3 tbsp. sugar and vanilla, beating until egg whites are creamy. Pour hot mixture slowly over egg whites, beating constantly. Cool slightly.

Pour into graham cracker shell. Cover with whipped cream and sprinkle with nuts. Chill well and serve.

Orange Delight

Cora Zello — Martinsburg, W. Va.

Dissolve 1 pkg. orange jello in 1 cup hot water. Add 1 pt. of vanilla ice cream, 1 small can crushed pinapple (drained), 2 cup oranges cut into sections or 2 cans mandarin oranges, 2 bananas (sliced), 1 small jar maraschino cherries (drained). Mix together and chill.

Sooner or later every good cook has to decide: Would she rather see the last spoonful go to _waste_ or _waist_?

Raspberry Delight

50 vanilla wafers
2 cups powdered sugar
1 cup nuts (chopped)
2 cups boiling water
1 ½ cups whipped cream
2 Tbsp. powdered sugar
¾ cup soft butter
1 3oz. pkg. cream cheese
2 small pkg. raspberry jello
2 10 oz. pkg. frozen raspberries

Dissolve jello in boiling water. Add thawed berries, including juice. Allow to thicken slightly. Set aside. Crumble vanilla wafers. Place ¾ of the wafers in bottom of 13 x 9 x 2 pan. Cream butter, powdered sugar and cream cheese. Put over crumbs in pan. Sprinkle with nuts. Whip cream with 2 Tbsp. sugar and spread over gelatin. Sprinkle with remaining crumbs. Chill.

Cherry Delight

L. Heuser   Luthersburg, Pa.

Beat 6 egg whites till stiff, add 3/4 tsp. cream of tartar. Add 2 cups sugar gradually. - Beat till stiff. Fold in 2 cups saltine crackers (crumbled by hand) into mix. Add 3/4 cups nuts, 2 tsp. vanilla. Bake at 350° for 25 min. Cool —

Prepare 2 pkgs. dream whip and spread on top - refrigerate. When cool spread 1 can of cherry pie filling on top.

Don't kick the person responsible for most of your troubles, unless you have a soft cushion on your chair!

Southern Pecan Pie

3 eggs
½ cup sugar
1 cup white Karo syrup
¼ cup butter
1 cup pecans (chopped)
⅛ tsp. salt
1 tsp. vanilla

    Beat eggs and add sugar, syrup, salt, vanilla and butter. Line a 9" pie tin with pastry. Pour pecans into crust and add mixture.

    Bake in 350° oven for 50 or 60 minutes.

    Pecans will rise to the top to form a crust.

Sisties' Pie

Sara Haney, P.C., Fl.

14 Saltine crackers
13 dates (2/3 cup chopped)
1 cup sugar
3 egg whites
1/2 cup nuts (chopped)
1/2 tsp. almond extract
1/2 tsp. salt

Roll crackers, chop dates and nuts and mix together.

Beat egg whites until stiff, add sugar extract and salt.

Fold into first mixture.

Bake in greased pie plate 30 min. at 325°

Serve with whipped cream and top with a cherry.

The Preacher's Wife

You may think it quite an easy task
   And just a pleasant life:
But really it takes a lot of grace
   To be a preachers wife.
She's supposed to be a paragon
   Without a fault in view.
A saint when in the parsonage
   As well as in the pew.

Her home must be a small hotel
   For folks that chance to roam,
And yet have peace and harmony—
   The perfect preacher's home!
Whenever groups are called to meet.
   Her presence must be there,
And yet the members all agree
   She should live a life of prayer.

Though hearing people's burdens,
   Their grief both night and day,
She's supposed to spread but sunshine
   To those along the way.
She must lend a sympathetic ear
   To every tale of woe,
And then forget about it,
   Lest it to others go.

Her children must be models rare
   Of quietness and poise,
But still stay on the level
   With other girls and boys.
You may think it quite an easy task,
   And just a pleasant life,
But really it takes a lot of grace
   To be a preacher's wife!

          — Author unknown —

Butternut Cake

2½ cups sifted flour
3 tsp. baking powder
1 tsp. salt
1½ cups sugar
1 cup milk
½ cup shortening
1 tsp. butternut flavoring
2 eggs, unbeaten

Sift flour and then measure. Add salt, B.P., and sugar and sift together. Mix shortening until smooth; add dry ingredients alternately with milk, add egg one at a time. Add flavoring.
Bake at 350° for 20-25 min.

Butternut Icing

1 box confectioners sugar
¾ stick margarine
1 (8 oz.) package cream cheese
1 cup chopped nuts
1 Tbsp. butternut flavoring

Mix all ingredients until well blended. Spread between layers and on top.

Pineapple Upside-down Cake

1 can of pineapple, drained
Melt 2 Tbsp. butter in a iron skillet over a slow fire and sprinkle evenly with ½ cup brown sugar. When sugar is melted remove from the stove and arrange the fruit over the sugar.

Separate 3 eggs, beat yolks until light and lemon colored. Continue beating while you add gradually ½ cup of sugar and ½ cup boiling water. Sift together 1 cup sugar, 1½ cups flour, 1 tsp. B.P. and ¼ tsp. salt.

Fold into above mixture. Then fold in 3 stiffly beaten egg whites.

Pour over fruit in skillit, bake in 350° oven for 45 minutes.

Turn out immediately!

Prune Cake

Zelma Frost, P.C., Jl.

3 eggs
1 cup wesson oil
1½ cups sugar
2 cups flour
1 tsp. soda
1 tsp. cin.
1 tsp. allspice
1 tsp. salt

1 cup buttermilk
1 cup prunes (cooked and seeded)
1 cup nuts
1 tsp. Vanilla

Mix dry ingredients and then oil and other ingredients.

Bake at 300° for 50 minutes.

Buttermilk Icing

1 cup sugar
½ cup buttermilk
½ tsp. soda
1 Tbsp. white syrup
½ cup butter (1 stick)
½ tsp. Vanilla

Boil about 4 minutes. Pour over the cake while the icing is still hot.

Red Velvet Cake

Cream: ½ cup shortening
1½ cups sugar
2 eggs

Make paste of: 2 oz. red cake coloring
2 Tbsp. cocoa

Add to sugar and shortening.
Mix 1 cup buttermilk and 1 tsp. salt.
Add alternately with:
2¼ cups flour
1 tsp. soda
1 tsp. vanilla

Bake 30 min. at 350° in 3 layers.

— Icing —

Cook until thick: 1 cup milk
3 Tbsp. flour

Cream: 1 cup butter
1 cup sugar
1 tsp. vanilla
until fluffy —
Blend into cooled flour mixture.
Spread on cake.

Beautiful Christmas Cake!

Fresh Apple Cake
Dodie Beach, P.C., Fl.

1¼ cup Wesson oil
3 eggs (well beaten)
2 cups sugar

Mix thoroughly. Add 3 cups chopped and peeled eating apples.
1 cup chopped pecans
2 tsp. vanilla
3 cups sifted flour
1 tsp. soda
1 tsp. salt

Sift together flour, soda, and salt 3 or 4 times. Pour in 2"×9" greased pans lined with waxed paper.

Put in cold oven — Bake 40-45 min. at 325°

Icing

Melt 1 stick margarine with 1 cup light brown sugar, Add ¼ cup canned cream — let boil 1 min. Let cool and add 1 tsp. vanilla.

Keeping Christmas

At Christmas, Herods of this world
   combine to confiscate
that star they never yet could see,
   flash swords of lust and hate.
Bright gold and frankincense for me —
   as stricken children wait?
Shekinah glow, Amazing Grace
   of God --- while many weep?

No, I must <u>share</u> -- on fields of earth —
   or never Christmas k<u>eep</u>!

        — Ruth Webber Shively —
            Irving, Texas

Golden Fruit Cake
Grandmom Pyle

2 cups light raisins
½ cup citron
1 cup pineapple
½ cup halved cherries
½ cup dates
1½ cups pecans
½ tsp. salt
2 tsp. B.P.
3 cups flour
1 cup margarine
1½ cups sugar
5 eggs
1 tsp. lemon flavor
1 cup orange or pineapple juice
1 jar preserves

Line pan with 2 thicknesses of greased brown paper and one thickness of greased waxed paper.

Bake 3 hours at 300°

Lane Cake

10 eggs
2 cups sugar
5 cups flour
1 cup milk
½ cup water

1 Tbsp. lemon flavor
4 tsp. B.P.
1½ c. shortening

Beat eggs until thin. Cream shortening and sugar, add eggs and continue to beat. Add milk and water in which the B.P. has been added. Add flour which has been sifted, then the flavoring. Bake in 3 layers.

Filling

5 egg yolks
⅓ cup grape juice
2 Tbsp. cornstarch
1 cup sugar
1 cup raisins   ⎫
1 cup nuts   ⎬ I grind these in meat chopper.
2 cups coconut   ⎭

Beat egg yolks, add sugar and juice. Add cornstarch dissolved in water. Cook in double boiler until thick. Remove from fire and add other ingredients. Spread ½ inch thick between layers and on top.
This is a special Christmas cake!

Happiness Cake

1 cup good thoughts
1 cup kind deeds
1 cup consideration for others
2 cups of sacrifice
2 cups of well-beaten faults
3 cups forgiveness

Mix thoroughly. Add tears of joy, sorrow and sympathy. Flavor with love and kindly service. Fold in 4 cups of prayer and faith. Blend well.

Fold into daily life. Bake well with the warmth of human kindness and serve with a smile, anytime. It will satisfy the hunger of starved souls.

Author Unknown

Pumpkin Cake Roll

3 eggs (whip 5 min.)
1 c. sugar (add gradually)
2/3 c. pumpkin
1 tsp. lemon juice
3/4 c. flour

1 tsp. B.P.
2 tsp. cin.
1 tsp. nutmeg
1 tsp. ginger
1/2 tsp. salt

Mix and spread in jelly roll pan that you have greased and lined with waxed paper. Sprinkle 1 cup chopped nuts on top.

Bake 15 – 20 min. in 375° oven.

Turn over on towel or waxed paper covered with confectioners sugar. Roll up and put in refrigerator to cool.

When cool unroll and put on filling and reroll.

— Filling —

1 cup confectioners sugar
6 oz. cream cheese
4 Tbsp. butter
1/2 tsp. vanilla

This can be made ahead of time and kept in the freezer until needed. It keeps well.

Serve it in slices with whipped cream on top. Delicious!

Sour Cream Cake

Sanford House, Milledgeville, Ga.

2 cups brown sugar
1 stick margarine
2 eggs
2 sqs. chocolate
2 cups flour
1 cup sour cream
1½ tsp. soda
¼ cup water

Melt butter, cream with sugar, add eggs. Beat until creamy, add melted chocolate, flour, sour cream to which soda is added, water and vanilla.

Put in 2 greased layer cake pans. Bake 20-25 min. at 350°.

Chocolate Icing

1 box confectioners sugar
1 stick margarine
3 sqs. chocolate
1 tsp. vanilla

Melt butter and chocolate over low flame. Put in mixer and add sugar which has been sifted. Add enough canned milk to make icing the consistency of heavy cream, add vanilla and spread on cake.

Plum Cake

Lucilla Hodges
Panama City, Fl.

Mix together:
- 2 cups self rising flour
- 1 tsp. cinnamon
- 1 tsp. cloves
- 2 cups sugar
- 1 cup Salad oil
- 3 eggs
- 2 jars plum baby food (strained)
- 1 cup chopped nuts

Bake 1 hour at 350° in a greased and floured tube pan.

Make a glaze of ½ cup conf. sugar and 3 tbsp. milk.

—"Bound in the bundle of life with the Lord thy God"— I Sam. 25:29

"Which holdeth our soul in life, and suffereth not our feet to be moved." Psalms 66:9

Carrot Cake

2 cups flour
2 tsp. baking powder
2 tsp. soda
1 tsp. salt
2 tsp. cinnamon
2 cups sugar
3 cups grated raw carrots
1 cup crisco
4 whole eggs (unbeaten)
½ cup chopped nuts

Sift flour, add dry ingredients. Mix sugar and shortening, cream well. Add carrots. Beat in eggs one at a time. Add dry ingredients and mix well.

Bake at 350° — makes 3 layers

Cream Cheese Icing

8 oz. cream cheese
1 box confectioners sugar
2 tsp. vanilla
1 stick margarine

Mix cheese and margarine. Cream until smooth. Add vanilla and sugar and mix well.

Coconut Pound Cake

Nora Lewis — Pensacola, Fla.

2 sticks Blue Bonnet margarine

1 stick butter

3 cups sugar

5 eggs

3 cups flour ⎫
½ tsp. salt ⎬ combine
1 tsp. B.P. ⎭

1 cup milk

1 pkg. frozen grated coconut (6 oz.) (thawed)

2 tsp. coconut flavoring

Cream margarine, butter, and sugar until real creamy and fluffy, add eggs one at a time, beating after each. Then add alternately in ⅓'s milk and flour mixture. Mix after each addition, then add coconut and flavoring.

Bake 1½ hours at 325° in a tube pan. May need 5 or 10 minutes longer.

Lemon Chess Pie

Opal Bradford, P.C., Fl.

2 cups sugar
1 Tbsp flour
1 Tbsp. cornmeal
¼ cup lemon juice
¼ cup milk
3 Tbsp. melted butter
4 eggs
grated lemons

Grate lemons used to make juice. Add sugar, meal and flour. Add liquid. Beat one egg at a time and add. Stir in melted butter and mix well.

Pour in 9" unbaked crust. Bake 1 hour, 20 min. at 350°

When softened butter or margarine is needed in a hurry, just grate the amount the recipe calls for, using coarse side.

Chocolate Cake

Margaret Blake — P.C., Fla.

2 cups flour ½ tsp. salt
2 cups sugar 4 tbsp. cocoa

Mix in bowl and set aside. Put ½ cup water, ½ cup cooking oil and 1 stick of margarine in saucepan and bring to a boil. Mix with dry ingredients.

After mixing add 2 eggs, ½ c. buttermilk, 1 tsp. soda and 1 tsp. vanilla. Pour into 10 x 14 baking pan. Bake at 350° — 20-25 min.

Frosting

Melt 1 stick margarine
Add 6 tbsp. milk
4 tbsp. cocoa
1 tsp. vanilla

Remove from heat and add:
1 box confectioners sugar
1 cup chopped nuts

Pour on cake while cake is hot.

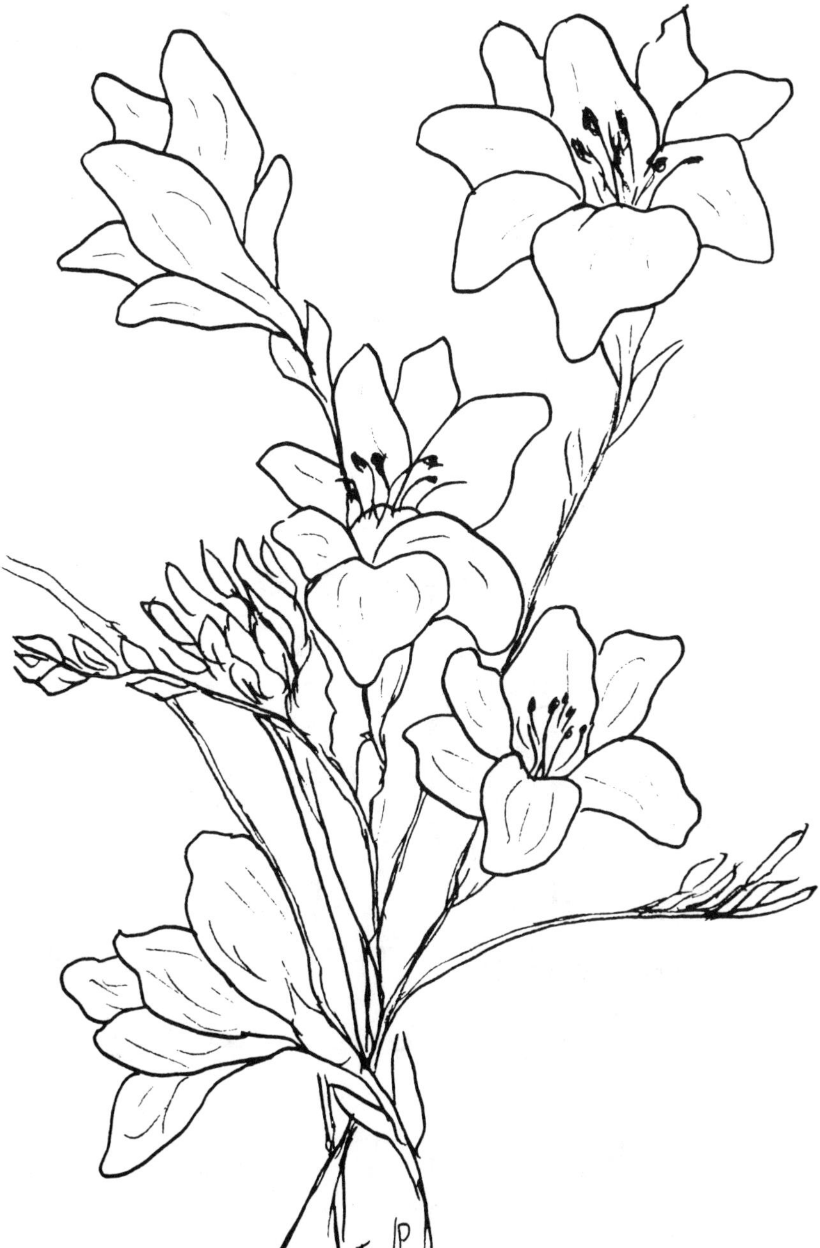
E.W.P.

Pound Cake

Lillian White

1 cup shortening (I use Crisco)
1 ¾ cups sugar
5 eggs
2 cups flour
5 tbsp. orange juice
1 tsp. vanilla

Cream sugar and shortening r*ea*l good.

Add eggs one at a time. With mixer on med. add one cup of the flour,
Then 2 tbsp orange juice,
½ cup flour
then the rest of orange juice and vanilla, Then ½ cup flour.

Pour into ungreased tube pan.

Bake 1 hour in 350° oven.

(If the eggs are large you may have to bake a little longer.)

Coconut Cake

Nell Helms, Ala.

1 Pkg. Duncan Hines Butter cake mix
Bake as directed in 4 layers.
When layers are cool frost with:

Frosting

2 pkgs. frozen coconut
1 cup sugar
1 cup sour cream
1 tsp. vanilla

This is also good if you add some cool whip to the top layer with the frosting.

"Pleasant words are as an honeycomb, sweet to the soul, and health to the bones."
Proverbs 16:24

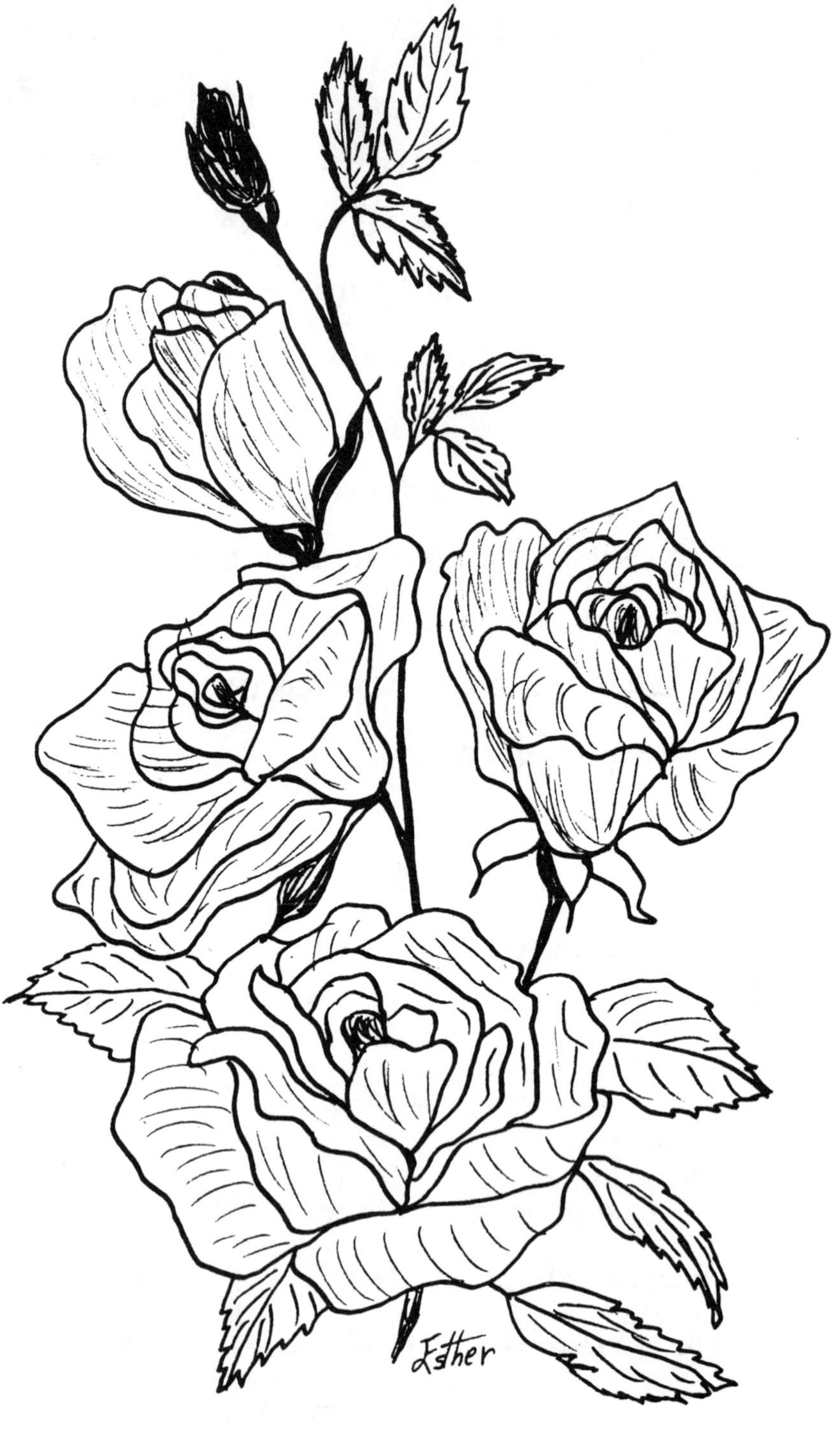
Esther

Poor Mans' Cake
Carrie A. Webber

1 Box seeded raisins
2 cups sugar
2 cups water
1 cup shortening
½ tsp salt
2 tsp. each cinnamon, nutmeg, allspice and cloves

Boil together 3 min., cool and add,
4 cups flour } sifted together
2 tsp. soda

Bake very slowly 1 hour. use 2 loaf pans.

This is a very old recipe given to me by my mother. It keeps well and gets better each day!

Pea-Pickin' Cake

Shirley Hartzog, P.C., Fl.

1 package yellow cake mix
1 can mandarin oranges with juice
1 cup wesson oil
4 eggs

Mix all above ingredients and bake at 350° for 30-35 minutes.

Bake in 3 layers.

Frosting

1 small box instant vanilla pudding
1 large (303) can crushed pineapple

Mix above ingredients. Fold in 9 oz. container of cool whip. Frost all 3 layers. Leave in refrigerator overnight.

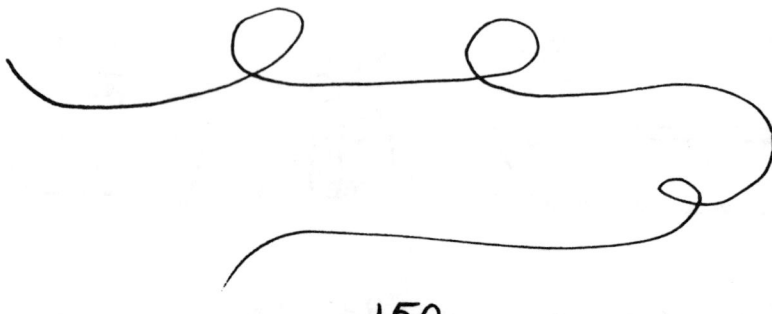

Bread and Butter Pickles

Sadie Davis
Panama City, Fl.

1 gal. sliced cucumbers
(add onions and bell peppers)
½ cup salt

Mix well and cover with ice for 3 hours.
Drain water and ice.

— Syrup —

5 cups sugar
5 cups vinegar
½ tsp. tumeric
½ tsp. ground cloves
2 tsp. mustard
2 Tbsp. celery seed

Bring to a boil. Add cucumbers. Scald but do not boil. Put in jars.
Makes 6 pints.

Pear Relish

Regina Howard, (Fla.)

- 12 lbs Pears
- 10 bell Peppers
- 10 medium onions
- 6 hot peppers
- 2 Tbsp. celery seed
- 2 tsp. salt
- 1 tsp. allspice
- 2 cups white vinegar
- 3 cups sugar

Grind pears, peppers, onions, and hot peppers, add remaining ingredients and cook 1 hour.

It is best to half this recipe and cook half of it at one time.

Makes about 12 pts.

"Keep thy tongue from evil, and thy lips from speaking guile."

Psalms 34:13

— Epitaph —

Here lies a poor woman
    Who always was tired,
She lived in a house
    Where help wasn't hired,
The last words she said
    Were, "Dear friends I am going
Where washing "aint" wanted,
    Nor sweeping nor sewing;
And everything there is
    Exact to my wishes,
For where folks don't eat
    There's no washing of dishes.
In heaven loud anthems
    Forever are ringing,
But having no voice
    I'll keep clear of the singing.
Don't mourn for me now,
    Don't mourn for me never,
I'm going to do nothing
    For ever and ever."

— Author Unknown —

Emerald House Group, Inc.
1 Chick Springs Road, Ste. 206
Greenville, SC 29609
1-800-209-8570

Please send me_____copies of ESTHER'S EDIBLES at $8.99 plus $3.75 postage and handling.

Enclosed is my check or money order for _____.

Name _____ Telephone _____

Address _____

City _____ State _____ Zip _____

Emerald House Group, Inc.
1 Chick Springs Road, Ste. 206
Greenville, SC 29609
1-800-209-8570

Please send me_____copies of ESTHER'S EDIBLES at $8.99 plus $3.75 postage and handling.

Enclosed is my check or money order for _____.

Name _____ Telephone _____

Address _____

City _____ State _____ Zip _____

Emerald House Group, Inc.
1 Chick Springs Road, Ste. 206
Greenville, SC 29609
1-800-209-8570

Please send me_____copies of ESTHER'S EDIBLES at $8.99 plus $3.75 postage and handling.

Enclosed is my check or money order for _____.

Name _____ Telephone _____

Address _____

City _____ State _____ Zip _____